Ramana Sahasram
A Thousand Ramanas

by Dr. H. Ramamoorthy

Published by
Society of Abidance in Truth (SAT)
1834 Ocean Street
Santa Cruz, CA 95060 USA
(831) 425-7287
www.SATRamana.org
email: sat@satramana.org

First Edition 1997
Second Edition 2023
ISBN 978-1-947154-32-2

Ramana Sahasram
A Thousand Ramanas

Composed in Sanskrit and translated into English by

Dr. H. Ramamoorthy

Acknowledgements

The SAT Temple expresses appreciation to:

Ganesh Sadasivan for inputting the text of this second edition and for proofreading,

Raman Muthukrishnan and Sangeeta Raman for proofreading

Sasvati for design and layout,

Nome for proofreading and inputting some of the text

All the members of SAT for their efforts and support toward the preservation and dissemination of the teachings bestowed by Bhagavan Sri Ramana Maharshi.

Introduction

On Namo Bhagavate Sri Ramanaya

"Ramana Sahasram" means "A Thousand Ramanas," which signifies a thousand ways Sri Ramana manifests or a thousand ways Sri Ramana is experienced. It pertains to his illimitable grace and all-transcendent wisdom. In reality, Ramana is only one, as Being is utterly indivisible. That is the Self, and that is Sri Bhagavan.

Who can describe the Absolute Self, the Supreme Being? One who realizes That is That. Thus is Bhagavan Sri Ramana Maharshi. Who can describe Bhagavan Sri Ramana Maharshi? Being inconceivable, he is ineffable.

Nevertheless, by His Grace, to express and inspire deep devotion, there are some who, steeped in wisdom, are humble masters of language able to express the inexpressible in such a magnificent manner as to plunge the reader or listener into the profound depths of Knowledge and launch one into absorption in immense bliss. The Ramana Sahasram, A Thousand Ramanas, is just such an expression of devotion and source of inspiration, intended for recitation and meditation.

Ramana Sahasram was composed in Sanskrit and translated into English in 1997 by Dr. H. Ramamoorthy. Although this book shares a few similarities with another book entitled Sri Ramana Sahasranama Stuti, they are completely independent works. This other list of a thousand names was composed many years ago by Jagadeeswara Sastri and translated into English, with commentary, by Sri A. R. Natarajan. This present book, Ramana Sahasram, with its emphasis upon non-duality as well as devotion, is ideal for recitation, contemplation, and meditation.

Here, in a thousand names for the nameless, is a description of a thousand attributes of the attributeless. May this be an offering to Sri Bhagavan.

रमणसहस्रम्

ramaṇa-sahasram

A Thousand Ramanas

ॐ

यस्य स्मरणमात्रेण
जन्मसंसारबन्धनात् ।
विमुच्यते नमस्तस्मै
भगवते रमणर्षये ॥

oṃ

yasya smaraṇa-mātreṇa
janma-saṃsāra-bandhanāt ।
vimucyate namas-tasmai
bhagavate ramaṇarṣaye ॥

Om
Just by thinking of whom
One is liberated from birth
and the bondage of samsara,
To that Sage Bhagavan Ramana, prostrations!

१ ॐ ओंकारनिलयाय रमणाय नमः

1 oṃ oṃkāra-nilayāya ramaṇāya namaḥ

Om! Prostrations to Ramana, who has the Pranava (Om) as the abode

२ ॐ भगवते रमणाय नमः

2 oṃ bhagavate ramaṇāya namaḥ

Om! Prostrations to Ramana, the Bhagavan

३ ॐ सद्गुरवे रमणाय नमः

3 oṃ sad-gurave ramaṇāya namaḥ

Om! Prostrations to Ramana, the true Guru

४ ॐ आत्मने रमणाय नमः

4 oṃ ātmane ramaṇāya namaḥ

Om! Prostrations to Ramana, the Self

५ ॐ अकाराय रमणाय नमः

5 oṃ akārāya ramaṇāya namaḥ

Om! Prostrations to Ramana, who is of the nature of 'a,' the first letter of Pranava

६ ॐ अखण्डसंविदाकाराय रमणाय नमः

6 oṃ akhaṇḍa-saṃvid-ākārāya ramaṇāya namaḥ

Om! Prostrations to Ramana, who is of the nature of the unbroken Consciousness

७ ॐ अकल्मषाय रमणाय नमः

7 oṃ akalmaṣāya ramaṇāya namaḥ

Om! Prostrations to Ramana, who is without any impurity

८ ॐ अखिलाय रमणाय नमः

8 oṃ akhilāya ramaṇāya namaḥ

Om! Prostrations to Ramana, who is the whole

९ ॐ अगणितमहिम्ने रमणाय नमः

9 oṃ agaṇita-mahimne ramaṇāya namaḥ

Om! Prostrations to Ramana with countless greatnesses

१० ॐ अगणितगुणाय रमणाय नमः

10 oṃ agaṇita-guṇāya ramaṇāya namaḥ

Om! Prostrations to Ramana with countless qualities

११ ॐ अग्रगण्याय रमणाय नमः

11 oṃ agra-gaṇyāya ramaṇāya namaḥ

Om! Prostrations to Ramana, who should be counted as the foremost

१२ ॐ अघौघमर्षणाय रमणाय नमः

12 oṃ aghaugha-marṣaṇāya ramaṇāya namaḥ

Om! Prostrations to Ramana, who forgives a whole mass of faults

१३ ॐ अंघ्रिजुषामनुग्रहाय रमणाय नमः

13 oṃ aṃghrijuṣām-anugrahāya ramaṇāya namaḥ

Om! Prostrations to Ramana, who blesses those who are devoted to his feet

१४ ॐ अक्षाकर्षणाय रमणाय नमः

14 oṃ akṣākarṣaṇāya ramaṇāya namaḥ

Om! Prostrations to Ramana, who captivates by the eye

१५ ॐ अक्षयाय रमणाय नमः

15 oṃ akṣayāya ramaṇāya namaḥ

Om! Prostrations to Ramana, who is decayless

१६ ॐ अक्षोभ्याय रमणाय नमः

16 oṃ akṣobhyāya ramaṇāya namaḥ

Om! Prostrations to Ramana, the imperturbable

१७ ॐ अक्षरमणमालाशोभिताय रमणाय नमः

17 oṃ akṣara-maṇa-mālā-śobhitāya ramaṇāya namaḥ

Om! Prostrations to Ramana, who shines with the marital garland of letters

१८ ॐ अचलोपमाय रमणाय नमः

18 oṃ acalopamāya ramaṇāya namaḥ

Om! Prostrations to Ramana, who is comparable to a mountain

१९ ॐ अचञ्चलाय रमणाय नमः

19 oṃ acañcalāya ramaṇāya namaḥ

Om! Prostrations to Ramana, who is unwavering

२० ॐ अचिन्त्यशक्तये रमणाय नमः

20 oṃ acintya-śaktaye ramaṇāya namaḥ

Om! Prostrations to Ramana, whose power cannot be imagined

२१ ॐ अच्युताय रमणाय नमः

21 oṃ acyutāya ramaṇāya namaḥ

Om! Prostrations to Ramana, who is firm, imperishable

२२ ॐ अचलपार्श्वाश्रमाय रमणाय नमः

22 oṃ acala-pārśv-āśramāya ramaṇāya namaḥ

Om! Prostrations to Ramana, who has his hermitage by the side of the mountain

२३ ॐ अजयाय रमणाय नमः

23 oṃ ajayāya ramaṇāya namaḥ

Om! Prostrations to Ramana, who is unconquerable

२४ ॐ अजिताय रमणाय नमः

24 oṃ ajitāya ramaṇāya namaḥ

Om! Prostrations to Ramana, who is unconquered

२५ ॐ अजराय रमणाय नमः

25 oṃ ajarāya ramaṇāya namaḥ

Om! Prostrations to Ramana, who never ages

२६ ॐ अज्ञहाय रमणाय नमः

26 oṃ ajñahāya ramaṇāya namaḥ

Om! Prostrations to Ramana, who destroys ignorance

२७ ॐ अज्ञानध्वान्तदीपिकाय रमणाय नमः

27 oṃ ajñāna-dhvānta-dīpikāya ramaṇāya namaḥ

Om! Prostrations to Ramana, the light that drives off [the darkness of] ignorance

२८ ॐ अण्णामलैवासिने रमणाय नमः

28 oṃ aṇṇāmalai-vāsine ramaṇāya namaḥ

Om! Prostrations to Ramana, the resident of Annamalai

२९ ॐ अतरंगाम्भोधिसदृशाय रमणाय नमः

29 oṃ ataraṃg-āmbhodhi-sadṛśāya ramaṇāya namaḥ

Om! Prostrations to Ramana, who is like a waveless ocean

३० ॐ अतिवर्णाय रमणाय नमः

30 oṃ ati-varṇāya ramaṇāya namaḥ

Om! Prostrations to Ramana, who transcends caste

३१ ॐ अतिदीप्ताय रमणाय नमः

31 oṃ ati-dīptāya ramaṇāya namaḥ

Om! Prostrations to Ramana, who is exceedingly bright

३२ ॐ अतीन्द्रियाय रमणाय नमः

32 oṃ atīndriyāya ramaṇāya namaḥ

Om! Prostrations to Ramana, who transcends the senses

३३ ॐ अतुलाय रमणाय नमः

33 oṃ atulāya ramaṇāya namaḥ

Om! Prostrations to Ramana, who is unequalled

३४ ॐ अत्यौषधाय रमणाय नमः

34 oṃ atyauṣadhāya ramaṇāya namaḥ

Om! Prostrations to Ramana, who is beyond herbs, medicine

३५ ॐ अदम्भाय रमणाय नमः

35 oṃ adambhāya ramaṇāya namaḥ

Om! Prostrations to Ramana, who is without deceit

३६ ॐ अद्भुतचर्याय रमणाय नमः

36 oṃ adbhuta-caryāya ramaṇāya namaḥ

Om! Prostrations to Ramana with wonderful conduct

३७ ॐ अद्भुतचारित्राय रमणाय नमः

37 oṃ adbhuta-cāritrāya ramaṇāya namaḥ

Om! Prostrations to Ramana with a wonderful history

३८ ॐ अद्वितीयाय रमणाय नमः

38 oṃ advitīyāya ramaṇāya namaḥ

Om! Prostrations to Ramana, who has no second

३९ ॐ अद्वैताचार्याय रमणाय नमः

39 oṃ advait-ācāryāya ramaṇāya namaḥ

Om! Prostrations to Ramana, Master of Advaita

४० ॐ अधर्षणाय रमणाय नमः

40 oṃ adharṣaṇāya ramaṇāya namaḥ

Om! Prostrations to Ramana without insolence

४१ ॐ अनघाय रमणाय नमः

41 oṃ anaghāya ramaṇāya namaḥ

Om! Prostrations to Ramana, who is faultless

४२ ॐ अनन्तनुताय रमणाय नमः

42 oṃ ananta-nutāya ramaṇāya namaḥ

Om! Prostrations to Ramana to whom endless people bow

४३ ॐ अनन्तरूपाय रमणाय नमः

43 oṃ ananta-rūpāya ramaṇāya namaḥ

Om! Prostrations to Ramana of endless forms

४४ ॐ अनन्तकल्याणगुणाय रमणाय नमः

44 oṃ ananta-kalyāṇa-guṇāya ramaṇāya namaḥ

Om! Prostrations to Ramana of endless excellent qualities

४५ ॐ अनसूयाय रमणाय नमः

45 oṃ anasūyāya ramaṇāya namaḥ

Om! Prostrations to Ramana with no jealousy

४६ ॐ अनादिने रमणाय नमः

46 oṃ anādine ramaṇāya namaḥ

Om! Prostrations to Ramana, who is originless

४७ ॐ अनादिनिधनाय रमणाय नमः

47 oṃ anādi-nidhanāya ramaṇāya namaḥ

Om! Prostrations to Ramana without birth or death

४८ ॐ अनाथनाथाय रमणाय नमः

48 oṃ anātha-nāthāya ramaṇāya namaḥ

Om! Prostrations to Ramana, the master for the masterless

४९ ॐ अनाथरक्षकाय रमणाय नमः

49 oṃ anātha-rakṣakāya ramaṇāya namaḥ

Om! Prostrations to Ramana, the protector for the protectorless

५० ॐ अनिन्दिताय रमणाय नमः

50 oṃ aninditāya ramaṇāya namaḥ

Om! Prostrations to Ramana, who cannot be faulted

५१ ॐ अनिवृत्तात्मने रमणाय नमः

51 oṃ anivṛtt-ātmane ramaṇāya namaḥ

Om! Prostrations to Ramana, the Self that has no return (being immanent)

५२ ॐ अनीताय रमणाय नमः

52 oṃ anītāya ramaṇāya namaḥ

Om! Prostrations to Ramana, who cannot be led

५३ ॐ अनुग्रहप्रदाय रमणाय नमः

53 oṃ anugraha-pradāya ramaṇāya namaḥ

Om! Prostrations to Ramana, who confers grace

५४ ॐ अनुदिनगिरिदर्शनाय रमणाय नमः

54 oṃ anudina-giri-darśanāya ramaṇāya namaḥ

Om! Prostrations to Ramana, who sees the mountain daily

५५ ॐ अन्तरात्मने रमणाय नमः

55 oṃ antar-ātmane ramaṇāya namaḥ

Om! Prostrations to Ramana, who is the inner Self

५६ ॐ अन्तर्हितात्मने रमणाय नमः

56 oṃ antar-hitātmane ramaṇāya namaḥ

Om! Prostrations to Ramana, who is inwardly beneficial

५७ ॐ अन्तःकरणप्रकाशकाय रमणाय नमः

57 oṃ antaḥ-karaṇa-prakāśakāya ramaṇāya namaḥ

Om! Prostrations to Ramana, who makes the inner instruments shine

५८ ॐ अन्तर्मुखसमाराध्याय रमणाय नमः

58 oṃ antar-mukha-samārādhyāya ramaṇāya namaḥ

Om! Prostrations to Ramana, who is well worshipped by an inward look

५९ ॐ अन्तस्तिमिरचण्डांशवे रमणाय नमः

59 oṃ antas-timira-caṇḍāṃśave ramaṇāya namaḥ

Om! Prostrations to Ramana, who is the sun that is the destroyer of the inner darkness

६० ॐ अपराय रमणाय नमः

60 oṃ aparāya ramaṇāya namaḥ

Om! Prostrations to Ramana, the lower aspect (too)

६१ ॐ अपूर्वशक्तये रमणाय नमः

61 oṃ apūrva-śaktaye ramaṇāya namaḥ

Om! Prostrations to Ramana, the power without a precedent

६२ ॐ अपूर्वज्ञानमार्गिणे रमणाय नमः

62 oṃ apūrva-jñāna-mārgiṇe ramaṇāya namaḥ

Om! Prostrations to Ramana, who shows the path without a precedent

६३ ॐ अप्पलगीतवित्तकाय रमणाय नमः

63 oṃ appala-gīta-vittakāya ramaṇāya namaḥ

Om! Prostrations to Ramana, the famous composer of the "appalam" song

६४ ॐ अप्रमेयाय रमणाय नमः

64 oṃ aprameyāya ramaṇāya namaḥ

Om! Prostrations to Ramana, who is not subject to a proof

६५ ॐ अभयहस्ताय रमणाय नमः

65 oṃ abhaya-hastāya ramaṇāya namaḥ

Om! Prostrations to Ramana with the hand signifying, "do not fear"

६६ ॐ अभयप्रदाय रमणाय नमः

66 oṃ abhaya-pradāya ramaṇāya namaḥ

Om! Prostrations to Ramana, who confers fearlessness

६७ ॐ अभिवाद्याय रमणाय नमः

67 oṃ abhivādyāya ramaṇāya namaḥ

Om! Prostrations to Ramana, who is to be offered respectful salutations

६८ ॐ अभिरामाय रमणाय नमः

68 oṃ abhirāmāya ramaṇāya namaḥ

Om! Prostrations to Ramana, who delights

६९ ॐ अमात्रे रमणाय नमः

69 oṃ amātre ramaṇāya namaḥ

Om! Prostrations to Ramana, who is without a measure, who is the silent last syllable of Pranava

७० ॐ अमराय रमणाय नमः

70 oṃ amarāya ramaṇāya namaḥ

Om! Prostrations to Ramana, the god, the deathless

७१ ॐ अमृताय रमणाय नमः

71 oṃ amṛtāya ramaṇāya namaḥ

Om! Prostrations to Ramana, the nectarine

७२ ॐ अमृतभाषिणे रमणाय नमः

72 oṃ amṛta-bhāṣiṇe ramaṇāya namaḥ

Om! Prostrations to Ramana of nectarine speech

७३ ॐ अमर्त्याय रमणाय नमः

73 oṃ amartyāya ramaṇāya namaḥ

Om! Prostrations to Ramana, the immortal

७४ ॐ अमिताय रमणाय नमः

74 oṃ amitāya ramaṇāya namaḥ

Om! Prostrations to Ramana, who is immeasurable

७५ ॐ अमितविक्रमाय रमणाय नमः

75 oṃ amita-vikramāya ramaṇāya namaḥ

Om! Prostrations to Ramana, whose power is immeasurable

७६ ॐ अमित्रजिते रमणाय नमः

76 oṃ amitra-jite ramaṇāya namaḥ

Om! Prostrations to Ramana, who wins over the unfriendly, those who have no friend

७७ ॐ अमुखाय रमणाय नमः

77 oṃ amukhāya ramaṇāya namaḥ

Om! Prostrations to Ramana, who is faceless

७८ ॐ अमूर्तये रमणाय नमः

78 oṃ amūrtaye ramaṇāya namaḥ

Om! Prostrations to Ramana, who is formless

७९ ॐ अरुषाय रमणाय नमः

79 oṃ aruṣāya ramaṇāya namaḥ

Om! Prostrations to Ramana, who is anger-less

८० ॐ अरुणाचलाकर्षितार्भकाय रमणाय नमः

80 oṃ aruṇācal-ākarṣit-ārbhakāya ramaṇāya namaḥ

Om! Prostrations to Ramana, the child who was attracted by Arunachala

८१ ॐ अरुणाचलात्मद्रष्टाय रमणाय नमः

81 oṃ aruṇācal-ātma-draṣṭāya ramaṇāya namaḥ

Om! Prostrations to Ramana, who saw Arunachala as the Self, in himself

८२ ॐ अरुणाचलनिवासाय रमणाय नमः

82 oṃ aruṇācala-nivāsāya ramaṇāya namaḥ

Om! Prostrations to Ramana, who is a resident of Arunachala

८३ ॐ अरुणाचलविहाराय रमणाय नमः

83 oṃ aruṇācala-vihārāya ramaṇāya namaḥ

Om! Prostrations to Ramana, who walks about on Arunachala

८४ ॐ अरुणाचलाय रमणाय नमः

84 oṃ aruṇācalāya ramaṇāya namaḥ

Om! Prostrations to Ramana, who is the Arunachala

८५ ॐ अलोकाय रमणाय नमः

85 oṃ alokāya ramaṇāya namaḥ

Om! Prostrations to Ramana, who is not of this world

८६ ॐ अवतारपूजिताय रमणाय नमः

86 oṃ avatāra-pūjitāya ramaṇāya namaḥ

Om! Prostrations to Ramana, who is worshipped as an incarnation

८७ ॐ अविद्यारहिताय रमणाय नमः

87 oṃ avidyā-rahitāya ramaṇāya namaḥ

Om! Prostrations to Ramana, who is without nescience

८८ ॐ अविद्याहरणाय रमणाय नमः

88 oṃ avidyā-haraṇāya ramaṇāya namaḥ

Om! Prostrations to Ramana, who takes away nescience

८९ ॐ अविच्युतनिजप्रज्ञाय रमणाय नमः

89 oṃ avicyuta-nija-prajñāya ramaṇāya namaḥ

Om! Prostrations to Ramana, who has not deviated from his own Consciousness

९० ॐ अव्यक्ताय रमणाय नमः

90 oṃ avyaktāya ramaṇāya namaḥ

Om! Prostrations to Ramana, who is the unmanifest (from which manifest creation has developed)

९१ ॐ अव्ययाय रमणाय नमः

91 oṃ avyayāya ramaṇāya namaḥ

Om! Prostrations to Ramana, the changeless

९२ ॐ असङ्गाय रमणाय नमः

92 oṃ asaṅgāya ramaṇāya namaḥ

Om! Prostrations to Ramana, the unattached

९३ ॐ अशक्यरहिताय रमणाय नमः

93 oṃ aśakya-rahitāya ramaṇāya namaḥ

Om! Prostrations to Ramana for whom there is nothing impossible

९४ ॐ अशेषजनवन्द्याय रमणाय नमः

94 oṃ aśeṣa-jana-vandyāya ramaṇāya namaḥ

Om! Prostrations to Ramana, who is to be worshipped by endless people

९५ ॐ अष्टसिद्ध्यतीताय रमणाय नमः

95 oṃ aṣṭa-siddhy-atītāya ramaṇāya namaḥ

Om! Prostrations to Ramana, who transcends the octet of siddhi-s

९६ ॐ असहायसहायाय रमणाय नमः

96 oṃ asahāya-sahāyāya ramaṇāya namaḥ

Om! Prostrations to Ramana, who is the friend of the friendless

९७ ॐ अहंकारनाशनाय रमणाय नमः

97 oṃ ahaṃkāra-nāśanāya ramaṇāya namaḥ

Om! Prostrations to Ramana, who destroys the ego

९८ ॐ आकाशकल्पाय रमणाय नमः

98 oṃ ākāśa-kalpāya ramaṇāya namaḥ

Om! Prostrations to Ramana, who is like space

९९ ॐ अहंब्रह्मास्मिवाक्यार्थाय रमणाय नमः

99 oṃ ahaṃ-brahmāsmi-vākyārthāya ramaṇāya namaḥ

Om! Prostrations to Ramana, who is the direct meaning of the statement 'I am Brahman'

१०० ॐ आत्मसाक्षात्कारबोधकाय रमणाय नमः

100 oṃ ātma-sākṣātkāra-bodhakāya ramaṇāya namaḥ

Om! Prostrations to Ramana, who taught Atmasakshatkara (direct awareness of the Self)

१०१ ॐ आत्मज्ञाय रमणाय नमः

101 oṃ ātma-jñāya ramaṇāya namaḥ

Om! Prostrations to Ramana, who knows the Self

१०२ ॐ आत्मानन्दाय रमणाय नमः

102 oṃ ātmānandāya ramaṇāya namaḥ

Om! Prostrations to Ramana, who is the bliss of the Self

१०३ ॐ आत्मविचाराय रमणाय नमः

103 oṃ ātma-vicārāya ramaṇāya namaḥ

Om! Prostrations to Ramana, who inquires into the Self

१०४ ॐ आत्मारामाय रमणाय नमः

104 oṃ ātmārāmāya ramaṇāya namaḥ

Om! Prostrations to Ramana, who reposes in the Self

१०५ ॐ आत्मरमणाय रमणाय नमः

105 oṃ ātma-ramaṇāya ramaṇāya namaḥ

Om! Prostrations to Ramana, who revels in the Self

१०६ ॐ आत्मस्थाय रमणाय नमः

106 oṃ ātma-sthāya ramaṇāya namaḥ

Om! Prostrations to Ramana, who is established in the Self

१०७ ॐ आत्मघोषणाय रमणाय नमः

107 oṃ ātma-ghoṣaṇāya ramaṇāya namaḥ

Om! Prostrations to Ramana, who proclaims the Self

१०८ ॐ आत्मनिष्ठाय रमणाय नमः

108 oṃ ātma-niṣṭhāya ramaṇāya namaḥ

Om! Prostrations to Ramana, who is established in the Self

१०९ ॐ आत्मवते रमणाय नमः

109 oṃ ātmavate ramaṇāya namaḥ

Om! Prostrations to Ramana, who has the Self

११० ॐ आत्मस्वरूपाय रमणाय नमः

110 oṃ ātma-svarūpāya ramaṇāya namaḥ

Om! Prostrations to Ramana, who is of the nature of the Self

१११ ॐ आत्मज्ञानप्रबोधकाय रमणाय नमः

111 oṃ ātma-jñāna-prabodhakāya ramaṇāya namaḥ

Om! Prostrations to Ramana, who awakens the Knowledge of the Self

११२ ॐ आत्मतत्त्वबोधकाय रमणाय नमः

112 oṃ ātma-tattva-bodhakāya ramaṇāya namaḥ

Om! Prostrations to Ramana, who teaches the truth of the Self

११३ ॐ आत्मविचारबोधकाय रमणाय नमः

113 oṃ ātma-vicāra-bodhakāya ramaṇāya namaḥ

Om! Prostrations to Ramana, who teaches inquiry into the Self

११४ ॐ आत्मयोगविशारदाय रमणाय नमः

114 oṃ ātma-yoga-viśāradāya ramaṇāya namaḥ

Om! Prostrations to Ramana, who is skilled in the yoga of the Self

११५ ॐ आत्मधर्मस्थापकाय रमणाय नमः

115 oṃ ātma-dharma-sthāpakāya ramaṇāya namaḥ

Om! Prostrations to Ramana, who has established the righteous path of the Self (atma-dharma)

११६ ॐ आत्मधर्मपरायणाय रमणाय नमः

116 oṃ ātma-dharma-parāyaṇāya ramaṇāya namaḥ

Om! Prostrations to Ramana, whose goal is atma-dharma (the path of the Self)

११७ ॐ आत्मयोगजिज्ञासूनामाश्रयाय रमणाय नमः

117 oṃ ātma-yoga-jijñāsūnām-āśrayāya ramaṇāya namaḥ

Om! Prostrations to Ramana, who is the refuge of those who seek to know atma-yoga

११८ ॐ आत्मकेन्द्रपूजिताय रमणाय नमः

118 oṃ ātma-kendra-pūjitāya ramaṇāya namaḥ

Om! Prostrations to Ramana, who is worshipped in the center of the Self

११९ ॐ आत्मसाम्राज्याभिषिक्ताय रमणाय नमः

119 oṃ ātma-sāmrājy-ābhiṣiktāya ramaṇāya namaḥ

Om! Prostrations to Ramana, who has been anointed in the empire of the Self

१२० ॐ आद्याय रमणाय नमः

120 oṃ ādyāya ramaṇāya namaḥ

Om! Prostrations to Ramana, the foremost

१२१ ॐ आद्यन्तरहिताय रमणाय नमः

121 oṃ ādyanta-rahitāya ramaṇāya namaḥ

Om! Prostrations to Ramana, who is without beginning or end

१२२ ॐ आदित्याय रमणाय नमः

122 oṃ ādityāya ramaṇāya namaḥ

Om! Prostrations to Ramana, the celestial luminary, the sun

१२३ ॐ आदर्शपुरुषाय रमणाय नमः

123 oṃ ādarśa-puruṣāya ramaṇāya namaḥ

Om! Prostrations to Ramana, the ideal person

१२४ ॐ आधारशक्तये रमणाय नमः

124 oṃ ādhāra-śaktaye ramaṇāya namaḥ

Om! Prostrations to Ramana, the power that supports

१२५ ॐ आधारनिलयाय रमणाय नमः

125 oṃ ādhāra-nilayāya ramaṇāya namaḥ

Om! Prostrations to Ramana, the abode that is the support

१२६ ॐ आधिव्याधिहराय रमणाय नमः

126 oṃ ādhi-vyādhi-harāya ramaṇāya namaḥ

Om! Prostrations to Ramana, who destroys the illness of the mind and the body

१२७ ॐ आनन्दाय रमणाय नमः

127 oṃ ānandāya ramaṇāya namaḥ

Om! Prostrations to Ramana, who is Bliss

१२८ ॐ आनन्ददाय रमणाय नमः

128 oṃ ānanda-dāya ramaṇāya namaḥ

Om! Prostrations to Ramana, who confers Bliss

१२९ ॐ आनन्दरूपाय रमणाय नमः

129 oṃ ānanda-rūpāya ramaṇāya namaḥ

Om! Prostrations to Ramana, who is Bliss personified

१३० ॐ आनन्दप्रसादकाय रमणाय नमः

130 oṃ ānanda-prasādakāya ramaṇāya namaḥ

Om! Prostrations to Ramana, who gives Bliss as his grace

१३१ ॐ आपद्बान्धवाय रमणाय नमः

131 oṃ āpad-bāndhavāya ramaṇāya namaḥ

Om! Prostrations to Ramana, the friend for one in danger

१३२ ॐ आपन्निवारकाय रमणाय नमः

132 oṃ āpan-nivārakāya ramaṇāya namaḥ

Om! Prostrations to Ramana, who forestalls danger

१३३ ॐ आप्ताय रमणाय नमः

133 oṃ āptāya ramaṇāya namaḥ

Om! Prostrations to Ramana, who is trustworthy

१३४ ॐ आर्तिहराय रमणाय नमः

134 oṃ ārti-harāya ramaṇāya namaḥ

Om! Prostrations to Ramana, who removes distress

१३५ ॐ आर्तत्राणपरायणाय रमणाय नम

135 oṃ ārta-trāṇa-parāyaṇāya ramaṇāya namaḥ

Om! Prostrations to Ramana, who is intent on saving those in distress

१३६ ॐ आर्याय रमणाय नमः

136 oṃ āryāya ramaṇāya namaḥ

Om! Prostrations to Ramana, the revered

१३७ ॐ आर्यावृत्तविरचित अरुणाचलपञ्चकद्रष्ट्रे रमणाय नमः

137 oṃ āryā-vṛtta-viracita aruṇācala-pañcaka-draṣṭre ramaṇāya namaḥ

Om! Prostrations to Ramana, the seer of the Arunachala Pancaka set out in the Arya meter

१३८ ॐ आशापाशनाशकाय रमणाय नमः

138 oṃ āśā-pāśa-nāśakāya ramaṇāya namaḥ

Om! Prostrations to Ramana, who destroys desire and attachment

१३९ ॐ आश्रितत्राणाय रमणाय नमः

139 oṃ āśrita-trāṇāya ramaṇāya namaḥ

Om! Prostrations to Ramana, who carries across those who take refuge in him

१४० ॐ आश्रितावनाय रमणाय नमः

140 oṃ āśrit-āvanāya ramaṇāya namaḥ

Om! Prostrations to Ramana, who protects those who take refuge in him

१४१ ॐ आश्रितपोषकाय रमणाय नमः

141 oṃ āśrita-poṣakāya ramaṇāya namaḥ

Om! Prostrations to Ramana, who nourishes those who take refuge in him

१४२ ॐ आश्रितपूजिताय रमणाय नमः

142 oṃ āśrita-pūjitāya ramaṇāya namaḥ

Om! Prostrations to Ramana, who is worshipped by those who take refuge in him

१४३ ॐ आश्चर्यरूपाय रमणाय नमः

143 oṃ āścarya-rūpāya ramaṇāya namaḥ

Om! Prostrations to Ramana of a wondrous nature

१४४ ॐ आश्चर्यप्रवर्तकाय रमणाय नमः

144 oṃ āścarya-pravartakāya ramaṇāya namaḥ

Om! Prostrations to Ramana, who spreads wonder

१४५ ॐ आह्लादवदनाय रमणाय नमः

145 oṃ āhlāda-vadanāya ramaṇāya namaḥ

Om! Prostrations to Ramana with a joyous face

१४६ ॐ इतिहासाय रमणाय नमः

146 oṃ itihāsāya ramaṇāya namaḥ

Om! Prostrations to Ramana, who is himself an epic

१४७ ॐ इनोदयप्रकाशाय रमणाय नमः

147 oṃ inodaya-prakāśāya ramaṇāya namaḥ

Om! Prostrations to Ramana, who shines like the sunrise

१४८ ॐ इन्दुमौलिनापितृमते रमणाय नमः

148 oṃ indu-maulinā-pitṛmate ramaṇāya namaḥ

Om! Prostrations to Ramana, who has as father the wearer of the crescent moon

१४९ ॐ ईड्याय रमणाय नमः

149 oṃ īḍyāya ramaṇāya namaḥ

Om! Prostrations to Ramana, who is to be adored

१५० ॐ ईतिबाधहराय रमणाय नमः

150 oṃ īti-bādha-harāya ramaṇāya namaḥ

Om! Prostrations to Ramana, who takes away the pain of distress

१५१ ॐ ईश्वराय रमणाय नमः

151 oṃ īśvarāya ramaṇāya namaḥ

Om! Prostrations to Ramana, the Lord

१५२ ॐ एषणत्रयवर्जिताय रमणाय नमः

152 oṃ eṣaṇa-traya-varjitāya ramaṇāya namaḥ

Om! Prostrations to Ramana devoid of the triple desires

१५३ ॐ ईर्ष्यारहिताय रमणाय नमः

153 oṃ īrṣyā-rahitāya ramaṇāya namaḥ

Om! Prostrations to Ramana, who is without envy

१५४ ॐ ईक्षणादिदीक्षातिरस्कृताय रमणाय नमः

154 oṃ īkṣaṇ-ādi-dīkṣā-tiraskṛtāya ramaṇāya namaḥ

Om! Prostrations to Ramana, who discards giving initiation by a look and such

१५५ ॐ उकाराय रमणाय नमः

155 oṃ ukārāya ramaṇāya namaḥ

Om! Prostrations to Ramana, who is of the nature of 'u', the second letter of Pranava

१५६ ॐ उत्कृष्टाय रमणाय नमः

156 oṃ utkṛṣṭāya ramaṇāya namaḥ

Om! Prostrations to Ramana, the eminent

१५७ ॐ उत्तमगुणसंपन्नाय रमणाय नमः

157 oṃ uttama-guṇa-saṃpannāya ramaṇāya namaḥ

Om! Prostrations to Ramana endowed with the best qualities

१५८ ॐ उत्तमाय रमणाय नमः

158 oṃ uttamāya ramaṇāya namaḥ

Om! Prostrations to Ramana, who is the best

१५९ ॐ उदाराय रमणाय नमः

159 oṃ udārāya ramaṇāya namaḥ

Om! Prostrations to Ramana, the generous one

१६० ॐ उदारकीर्तये रमणाय नमः

160 oṃ udāra-kīrtaye ramaṇāya namaḥ

Om! Prostrations to Ramana with far-flung fame, one famous for generosity

१६१ ॐ उद्दीप्तनयनाय रमणाय नमः

161 oṃ uddīpta-nayanāya ramaṇāya namaḥ

Om! Prostrations to Ramana with shining eyes

१६२ ॐ उद्दामवैभवाय रमणाय नमः

162 oṃ uddāma-vaibhavāya ramaṇāya namaḥ

Om! Prostrations to Ramana, whose glory is resounding

१६३ ॐ उदासीनाय रमणाय नमः

163 oṃ udāsīnāya ramaṇāya namaḥ

Om! Prostrations to Ramana, who is indifferent

१६४ ॐ उन्मनाय रमणाय नमः

164 oṃ unmanāya ramaṇāya namaḥ

Om! Prostrations to Ramana with his mind absent

१६५ ॐ उन्मेषाय रमणाय नमः

165 oṃ unmeṣāya ramaṇāya namaḥ

Om! Prostrations to Ramana with eyelids open

१६६ ॐ उपलब्धिने रमणाय नमः

166 oṃ upalabdhine ramaṇāya namaḥ

Om! Prostrations to Ramana possessed of Knowledge

१६७ ॐ उपशान्ताय रमणाय नमः

167 oṃ upaśāntāya ramaṇāya namaḥ

Om! Prostrations to Ramana extremely peaceful

१६८ ॐ उपद्रवहरणाय रमणाय नमः

168 oṃ upadrava-haraṇāya ramaṇāya namaḥ

Om! Prostrations to Ramana, who removes troubles

१६९ ॐ उपाधिरहिताय रमणाय नमः

169 oṃ upādhi-rahitāya ramaṇāya namaḥ

Om! Prostrations to Ramana without conditionings

१७० ॐ उपाधिनिवर्तकाय रमणाय नमः

170 oṃ upādhi-nivartakāya ramaṇāya namaḥ

Om! Prostrations to Ramana, who prevents limitations

१७१ ॐ उपदेष्ट्रे रमणाय नमः

171 oṃ upadeṣṭre ramaṇāya namaḥ

Om! Prostrations to Ramana, who gives upadesa, spiritual instruction

१७२ ॐ उपदेशसारविधायकाय रमणाय नमः

172 oṃ upadeśa-sāra-vidhāyakāya ramaṇāya namaḥ

Om! Prostrations to Ramana, the author of Upadesasara

१७३ ॐ उल्लङ्घितसंप्रदायाय रमणाय नमः

173 oṃ ullaṅghita-saṃpradāyāya ramaṇāya namaḥ

Om! Prostrations to Ramana, who steps across the frontiers of tradition

१७४ ॐ ऊर्जगतिदायकाय रमणाय नमः

174 oṃ ūrja-gati-dāyakāya ramaṇāya namaḥ

Om! Prostrations to Ramana, who confers the high path

१७५ ॐ ऊर्जस्वनाय रमणाय नमः

175 oṃ ūrjasvanāya ramaṇāya namaḥ

Om! Prostrations to Ramana with a mighty voice, who makes a mighty sound

१७६ ॐ ऊर्जिताय रमणाय नमः

176 oṃ ūrjitāya ramaṇāya namaḥ

Om! Prostrations to Ramana, who is powerful

१७७ ॐ ऊर्जितोदाराय रमणाय नमः

177 oṃ ūrjitodārāya ramaṇāya namaḥ

Om! Prostrations to Ramana, whose generosity is established, of high repute

१७८ ॐ ऊर्जस्वलाय रमणाय नमः

178 oṃ ūrjasvalāya ramaṇāya namaḥ

Om! Prostrations to Ramana, who is effulgent

१७९ ॐ ऊर्ध्वाधविवर्जिताय रमणाय नमः

179 oṃ ūrdhv-ādha-vivarjitāya ramaṇāya namaḥ

Om! Prostrations to Ramana devoid of above and below

१८० ॐ ऋभुगीताप्रदर्शकाय रमणाय नमः

180 oṃ ṛbhu-gītā-pradarśakāya ramaṇāya namaḥ

Om! Prostrations to Ramana, who has revealed the Ribhu Gita

१८१ ॐ ऋगादिचतुर्वेदस्वरूपाय रमणाय नमः

181 oṃ ṛg-ādi-catur-veda-svarūpāya ramaṇāya namaḥ

Om! Prostrations to Ramana, who is of the nature of the four Veda-s such as Rg

१८२ ॐ ऋजुकराय रमणाय नमः

182 oṃ ṛju-karāya ramaṇāya namaḥ

Om! Prostrations to Ramana, who sets right, corrects

१८३ ॐ ऋजुमार्गप्रदर्शकाय रमणाय नमः

183 oṃ ṛju-mārga-pradarśakāya ramaṇāya namaḥ

Om! Prostrations to Ramana, who shows the right way

१८४ ॐ ऋणत्रयविवर्जिताय रमणाय नमः

184 oṃ ṛṇa-traya-vivarjitāya ramaṇāya namaḥ

Om! Prostrations to Ramana, who is without the triad of debts (to gods, sages, and forefathers)

१८५ ॐ ऋणत्रयविमोचनाय रमणाय नमः

185 oṃ ṛṇa-traya-vimocanāya ramaṇāya namaḥ

Om! Prostrations to Ramana, who gives release from the triad of debts

१८६ ॐ ऋषिपुङ्गवाय रमणाय नमः

186 oṃ ṛṣi-puṅgavāya ramaṇāya namaḥ

Om! Prostrations to Ramana, the exalted among sages

१८७ ॐ एकाकिने रमणाय नमः

187 oṃ ekākine ramaṇāya namaḥ

Om! Prostrations to Ramana, who is by himself

१८८ ॐ एकान्ताय रमणाय नमः

188 oṃ ekāntāya ramaṇāya namaḥ

Om! Prostrations to Ramana, who is in a secluded place

१८९ ॐ एकात्मपञ्चकाय रमणाय नमः

189 oṃ ekātma-pañcakāya ramaṇāya namaḥ

Om! Prostrations to Ramana, who composed the Ekatma Pancaka

१९० ॐ ऐश्वर्याय रमणाय नमः

190 oṃ aiśvaryāya ramaṇāya namaḥ

Om! Prostrations to Ramana, who has Lordliness

१९१ ॐ ओंकारस्वरूपाय रमणाय नमः

191 oṃ oṃkāra-svarūpāya ramaṇāya namaḥ

Om! Prostrations to Ramana, who is of the nature of Omkara

१९२ ॐ ओंकारगात्राय रमणाय नमः

192 oṃ oṃkāra-gātrāya ramaṇāya namaḥ

Om! Prostrations to Ramana, who is the embodiment of Om

१९३ ॐ ओंकारपरमार्थाय रमणाय नमः

193 oṃ oṃkāra-paramārthāya ramaṇāya namaḥ

Om! Prostrations to Ramana, who is the great meaning of Om, one who is the Reality

१९४ ॐ औदार्याय रमणाय नमः

194 oṃ audāryāya ramaṇāya namaḥ

Om! Prostrations to Ramana, who is generous

१९५ ॐ कमनीयाय रमणाय नमः

195 oṃ kamanīyāya ramaṇāya namaḥ

Om! Prostrations to Ramana, who is charming

१९६ ॐ कमनीयचारित्राय रमणाय नमः

196 oṃ kamanīya-cāritrāya ramaṇāya namaḥ

Om! Prostrations to Ramana, whose history is charming

१९७ ॐ कमण्डलुधरसुधाब्धये रमणाय नमः

197 oṃ kamaṇḍalu-dhara-sudhābdhaye ramaṇāya namaḥ

Om! Prostrations to Ramana, who carries in a kamandalu an ocean of nectar

१९८ ॐ कमलपत्रविशाललोचनाय रमणाय नमः

198 oṃ kamala-patra-viśāla-locanāya ramaṇāya namaḥ

Om! Prostrations to Ramana, whose eyes are large as lotus-petals

१९९ ॐ करुणाक्षाय रमणाय नमः

199 oṃ karuṇākṣāya ramaṇāya namaḥ

Om! Prostrations to Ramana, who has compassionate eyes

२०० ॐ करुणालयाय रमणाय नमः

200 oṃ karuṇālayāya ramaṇāya namaḥ

Om! Prostrations to Ramana, who is the abode of compassion

२०१ ॐ करुणासागराय रमणाय नमः

201 oṃ karuṇā-sāgarāya ramaṇāya namaḥ

Om! Prostrations to Ramana, the ocean of compassion

२०२ ॐ करुणानिधये रमणाय नमः

202 oṃ karuṇā-nidhaye ramaṇāya namaḥ

Om! Prostrations to Ramana, the treasure of compassion

२०३ ॐ करुणारससंपूर्णाय रमणाय नमः

203 oṃ karuṇā-rasa-saṃpūrṇāya ramaṇāya namaḥ

Om! Prostrations to Ramana filled with the essence of compassion

२०४ ॐ करुणापूर्णहृदयाय रमणाय नमः

204 oṃ karuṇā-pūrṇa-hṛdayāya ramaṇāya namaḥ

Om! Prostrations to Ramana with a heart full of compassion

२०५ ॐ कर्मसर्वबन्धविमोचनाय रमणाय नमः

205 oṃ karma-sarva-bandha-vimocanāya ramaṇāya namaḥ

Om! Prostrations to Ramana, who is released from all bondage of karma

२०६ ॐ कर्मध्वंसिने रमणाय नमः

206 oṃ karma-dhvaṃsine ramaṇāya namaḥ

Om! Prostrations to Ramana, who destroys karma

२०७ ॐ कल्पतरवे रमणाय नमः

207 oṃ kalpa-tarave ramaṇāya namaḥ

Om! Prostrations to Ramana, the wish-fulfilling tree

२०८ ॐ कल्मषध्वंसिने रमणाय नमः

208 oṃ kalmaṣa-dhvaṃsine ramaṇāya namaḥ

Om! Prostrations to Ramana, who destroys all darkness

२०९ ॐ कविकुञ्जराय रमणाय नमः

209 oṃ kavi-kuñjarāya ramaṇāya namaḥ

Om! Prostrations to Ramana, the eminent among poets

२१० ॐ कविवरस्तुताय रमणाय नमः

210 oṃ kavi-vara-stutāya ramaṇāya namaḥ

Om! Prostrations to Ramana praised by the best of poets

२११ ॐ कामनाशनाय रमणाय नमः

211 oṃ kāma-nāśanāya ramaṇāya namaḥ

Om! Prostrations to Ramana, who destroys desire

२१२ ॐ क्रोधनाशनाय रमणाय नमः

212 oṃ krodha-nāśanāya ramaṇāya namaḥ

Om! Prostrations to Ramana, who destroys anger

२१३ ॐ क्लेशनाशनाय रमणाय नमः

213 oṃ kleśa-nāśanāya ramaṇāya namaḥ

Om! Prostrations to Ramana, who destroys anguish

२१४ ॐ कार्यकारणनिर्मुक्ताय रमणाय नमः

214 oṃ kārya-kāraṇa-nirmuktāya ramaṇāya namaḥ

Om! Prostrations to Ramana, who is free from cause and effect

२१५ ॐ कारणोद्भवाय रमणाय नमः

215 oṃ kāraṇodbhavāya ramaṇāya namaḥ

Om! Prostrations to Ramana, who is born for a cause

२१६ ॐ कालाय रमणाय नमः

216 oṃ kālāya ramaṇāya namaḥ

Om! Prostrations to Ramana, who is time, the destroyer, Siva

२१७ ॐ कालघ्ने रमणाय नमः

217 oṃ kālaghne ramaṇāya namaḥ

Om! Prostrations to Ramana, who destroys time

२१८ ॐ कालकालाय रमणाय नमः

218 oṃ kāla-kālāya ramaṇāya namaḥ

Om! Prostrations to Ramana, who is the destroyer of the god of death

२१९ ॐ कालातीताय रमणाय नमः

219 oṃ kālātītāya ramaṇāya namaḥ

Om! Prostrations to Ramana, who transcends time

२२० ॐ काव्यालापविनोदिने रमणाय नमः

220 oṃ kāvyālāpa-vinodine ramaṇāya namaḥ

Om! Prostrations to Ramana, who delights in poetic discussion

२२१ ॐ काष्टमौनाय रमणाय नमः

221 oṃ kāṣṭa-maunāya ramaṇāya namaḥ

Om! Prostrations to Ramana, who is silent like a log of wood

२२२ ॐ कुमाराय रमणाय नमः

222 oṃ kumārāya ramaṇāya namaḥ

Om! Prostrations to Ramana, the youth (who was indeed a master)

२२३ ॐ कुमारगुरवे रमणाय नमः

223 oṃ kumāra-gurave ramaṇāya namaḥ

Om! Prostrations to Ramana, the boy who is a guru

२२४ ॐ कुमारस्वामिने रमणाय नमः

224 oṃ kumāra-svāmine ramaṇāya namaḥ

Om! Prostrations to Ramana, the boy who is a master

२२५ ॐ कुशाग्रधिये रमणाय नमः

225 oṃ kuśāgra-dhiye ramaṇāya namaḥ

Om! Prostrations to Ramana, with an intellect sharp like the edge of dry grass

२२६ ॐ कूटस्थाय रमणाय नमः

226 oṃ kūṭasthāya ramaṇāya namaḥ

Om! Prostrations to Ramana, the immovable (like space)

२२७ ॐ कृपापूर्णाय रमणाय नमः

227 oṃ kṛpā-pūrṇāya ramaṇāya namaḥ

Om! Prostrations to Ramana, filled with Grace

२२८ ॐ कृपार्णवाय रमणाय नमः

228 oṃ kṛpārṇavāya ramaṇāya namaḥ

Om! Prostrations to Ramana, the ocean of Grace

२२९ ॐ कृपानिधये रमणाय नमः

229 oṃ kṛpā-nidhaye ramaṇāya namaḥ

Om! Prostrations to Ramana, the treasure of Grace

२३० ॐ कृतकृत्याय रमणाय नमः

230 oṃ kṛta-kṛtyāya ramaṇāya namaḥ

Om! Prostrations to Ramana, who has completed his duties

२३१ ॐ केन्द्रपूजिताय रमणाय नमः

231 oṃ kendra-pūjitāya ramaṇāya namaḥ

Om! Prostrations to Ramana, who is worshipped in the center(s)

२३२ ॐ केवलाय रमणाय नमः

232 oṃ kevalāya ramaṇāya namaḥ

Om! Prostrations to Ramana, the Ramana that alone is

२३३ ॐ कैवल्यपददायिने रमणाय नमः

233 oṃ kaivalya-pada-dāyine ramaṇāya namaḥ

Om! Prostrations to Ramana, who confers the state of being Kaivalya (being the Lone)

२३४ ॐ कोऽहंमन्त्रऋषये रमणाय नमः

234 oṃ ko'haṃ-mantra-ṛṣaye ramaṇāya namaḥ

Om! Prostrations to Ramana, the seer of the "mantra" "Who am I?"

२३५ ॐ ख्याताय रमणाय नमः

235 oṃ khyātāya ramaṇāya namaḥ

Om! Prostrations to Ramana, who is well-known, famous

२३६ ॐ गंभीराय रमणाय नमः

236 oṃ gaṃbhīrāya ramaṇāya namaḥ

Om! Prostrations to Ramana, who is majestic

२३७ ॐ गतये रमणाय नमः

237 oṃ gataye ramaṇāya namaḥ

Om! Prostrations to Ramana, who is the path

२३८ ॐ गतिदाय रमणाय नमः

238 oṃ gati-dāya ramaṇāya namaḥ

Om! Prostrations to Ramana, who shows the path

२३९ ॐ गद्यपद्यप्रियाय रमणाय नमः

239 oṃ gadya-padya-priyāya ramaṇāya namaḥ

Om! Prostrations to Ramana, who loves prose and poetry

२४० ॐ गणनीयगुणाय रमणाय नमः

240 oṃ gaṇanīya-guṇāya ramaṇāya namaḥ

Om! Prostrations to Ramana, whose qualities should be revered

२४१ ॐ गणनीयचरित्राय रमणाय नमः

241 oṃ gaṇanīya-caritrāya ramaṇāya namaḥ

Om! Prostrations to Ramana, whose history should be revered

२४२ ॐ गानप्रियाय रमणाय नमः

242 oṃ gāna-priyāya ramaṇāya namaḥ

Om! Prostrations to Ramana, who likes music and singing

२४३ ॐ गणपतिमुनिकाव्यदेवाय रमणाय नमः

243 oṃ gaṇapati-muni-kāvya-devāya ramaṇāya namaḥ

Om! Prostrations to Ramana, who is the god of the poetry of Ganapati Muni

२४४ ॐ गणेशमुनिभृङ्गेन सेवितांघ्रि सरोरुहाय रमणाय नमः

244 oṃ gaṇeśa-muni-bhṛṅgena sevitāṃghri saroruhāya ramaṇāya namaḥ

Om! Prostrations to Ramana with his lotus feet served by the bee that is Ganapati Muni

२४५ ॐ गिरिचराय रमणाय नमः

245 oṃ giri-carāya ramaṇāya namaḥ

Om! Prostrations to Ramana, who strides over the mountains

२४६ ॐ गिरीवप्रदक्षिण्याय रमणाय नमः

246 oṃ girīva-pradakṣiṇyāya ramaṇāya namaḥ

Om! Prostrations to Ramana, who is to be circumambulated like a mountain

२४७ ॐ गिरिभूतज्वालाय रमणाय नमः

247 oṃ giri-bhūta-jvālāya ramaṇāya namaḥ

Om! Prostrations to Ramana, the fire-column that became a mountain

२४८ ॐ गुणाकराय रमणाय नमः

248 oṃ guṇā-karāya ramaṇāya namaḥ

Om! Prostrations to Ramana, the mine of good qualities

२४९ ॐ गुणौषधाय नमः

249 oṃ guṇauṣadhāya namaḥ

Om! Prostrations to Ramana with qualities that are a medicament, herb

२५० ॐ गुणवर्धनाय रमणाय नमः

250 oṃ guṇa-vardhanāya ramaṇāya namaḥ

Om! Prostrations to Ramana, who nourishes good qualities

२५१ ॐ गुणनिधये रमणाय नमः

251 oṃ guṇa-nidhaye ramaṇāya namaḥ

Om! Prostrations to Ramana, the treasure of good qualities

२५२ ॐ गुणार्णवाय रमणाय नमः

252 oṃ guṇārṇavāya ramaṇāya namaḥ

Om! Prostrations to Ramana, the ocean of good qualities

२५३ ॐ गुणश्रेष्ठाय रमणाय नमः

253 oṃ guṇa-śreṣṭhāya ramaṇāya namaḥ

Om! Prostrations to Ramana distinguished for good qualities

२५४ ॐ गुणज्ञाय रमणाय नमः

254 oṃ guṇa-jñāya ramaṇāya namaḥ

Om! Prostrations to Ramana, who appreciates good qualities

२५५ ॐ गुणात्मने रमणाय नमः

255 oṃ guṇātmane ramaṇāya namaḥ

Om! Prostrations to Ramana, who has in him good qualities

२५६ ॐ गुणातीताय रमणाय नमः

256 oṃ guṇātītāya ramaṇāya namaḥ

Om! Prostrations to Ramana, who transcends qualities

२५७ ॐ गुरवे रमणाय नमः

257 oṃ gurave ramaṇāya namaḥ

Om! Prostrations to Ramana, the Guru

२५८ ॐ गुरुमूर्तये रमणाय नमः

258 oṃ guru-mūrtaye ramaṇāya namaḥ

Om! Prostrations to Ramana, the embodiment of the Guru, Guru with form

२५९ ॐ गुरुमूर्तगुरुमूर्तये रमणाय नमः

259 oṃ gurumūrta-gurumūrtaye ramaṇāya namaḥ

Om! Prostrations to Ramana, the Guru with form [who stayed] at Gurumurtam

२६० ॐ गुरुवराय रमणाय नमः

260 oṃ guru-varāya ramaṇāya namaḥ

Om! Prostrations to Ramana, the worthy Guru

२६१ ॐ गुरुश्रेष्ठाय रमणाय नमः

261 oṃ guru-śreṣṭhāya ramaṇāya namaḥ

Om! Prostrations to Ramana, the best among Gurus

२६२ ॐ गुहाय रमणाय नमः

262 oṃ guhāya ramaṇāya namaḥ

Om! Prostrations to Ramana, who is the cave [of the heart]

२६३ ॐ गुहावासिने रमणाय नमः

263 oṃ guhā-vāsine ramaṇāya namaḥ

Om! Prostrations to Ramana, who resided in a cave (in Annamalai), resides in the cave [of the heart]

२६४ ॐ गोलक्ष्मीनाथाय रमणाय नमः

264 oṃ go-lakṣmī-nāthāya ramaṇāya namaḥ

Om! Prostrations to Ramana, the Lord of the earth and wealth, the Lord of the cow Lakshmi

२६५ ॐ गोप्रियाय रमणाय नमः

265 oṃ go-priyāya ramaṇāya namaḥ

Om! Prostrations to Ramana, who loves cows (also one who is loved by the cows)

२६६ ॐ गोपालाय रमणाय नमः

266 oṃ go-pālāya ramaṇāya namaḥ

Om! Prostrations to Ramana, the ruler of the cows, of the earth

२६७ ॐ चतुर्वेदविदे रमणाय नमः

267 oṃ catur-veda-vide ramaṇāya namaḥ

Om! Prostrations to Ramana, who knows the four Veda-s

२६८ ॐ चतुराय रमणाय नमः

268 oṃ caturāya ramaṇāya namaḥ

Om! Prostrations to Ramana, the clever one

२६९ ॐ चञ्चलनाशनाय रमणाय नमः

269 oṃ cañcala-nāśanāya ramaṇāya namaḥ

Om! Prostrations to Ramana, who destroys uncertainty, wavering

२७० ॐ चन्द्रार्ककोटिसदृशाननाय रमणाय नमः

270 oṃ candrārka-koṭi-sadṛś-ānanāya ramaṇāya namaḥ

Om! Prostrations to Ramana with a face resembling ten million moons and suns

२७१ ॐ चरितामृतसागराय रमणाय नमः

271 oṃ caritāmṛta-sāgarāya ramaṇāya namaḥ

Om! Prostrations to Ramana with a history that is an ocean of nectar

२७२ ॐ चत्वारिंशत्सद्दर्शनश्लोकिने रमणाय नमः

272 oṃ catvāriṃśat-saddarśana-ślokine ramaṇāya namaḥ

Om! Prostrations to Ramana, who composed the Saddarshana of forty verses

२७३ ॐ चन्द्रिकासितहासश्रीमण्डितानन्द मण्डलाय रमणाय नमः

273 oṃ candrikā-sita-hāsa-śrī-maṇḍit-ānanda maṇḍalāya ramaṇāya namaḥ

Om! Prostrations to Ramana, with an orb of bliss shining with the moonlight of his auspicious laughter

२७४ ॐ चारुरूपाय रमणाय नमः

274 oṃ cāru-rūpāya ramaṇāya namaḥ

Om! Prostrations to Ramana, with a charming nature, form

२७५ ॐ चरुहासाय रमणाय नमः

275 oṃ caru-hāsāya ramaṇāya namaḥ

Om! Prostrations to Ramana, who laughs charmingly

२७६ ॐ चारुशीलाय रमणाय नमः

276 oṃ cāru-śīlāya ramaṇāya namaḥ

Om! Prostrations to Ramana, whose conduct is charming

२७७ ॐ चित्स्वरूपाय रमणाय नमः

277 oṃ cit-svarūpāya ramaṇāya namaḥ

Om! Prostrations to Ramana of the nature of Consciousness

२७८ ॐ चिदानन्दाय रमणाय नमः

278 oṃ cid-ānandāya ramaṇāya namaḥ

Om! Prostrations to Ramana in the bliss of Consciousness

२७९ ॐ चिन्मयाय रमणाय नमः

279 oṃ cin-mayāya ramaṇāya namaḥ

Om! Prostrations to Ramana full of Consciousness

२८० ॐ चिन्मुद्रिणे रमणाय नमः

280 oṃ cin-mudriṇe ramaṇāya namaḥ

Om! Prostrations to Ramana holding the gesture of Consciousness (cinmudra)

२८१ ॐ चिदाभासाय रमणाय नमः

281 oṃ cid-ābhāsāya ramaṇāya namaḥ

Om! Prostrations to Ramana, who is an image of Consciousness

२८२ ॐ चित्तवृत्तिनाशनाय रमणाय नमः

282 oṃ citta-vṛtti-nāśanāya ramaṇāya namaḥ

Om! Prostrations to Ramana, who destroys the thought mode

२८३ ॐ चित्तवृत्तिशून्यप्रदर्शकाय रमणाय नमः

283 oṃ citta-vṛtti-śūnya-pradarśakāya ramaṇāya namaḥ

Om! Prostrations to Ramana, who reveals the non-existence of the thought mode

२८४ ॐ चूर्णिताखिलभ्रमाय रमणाय नमः

284 oṃ cūrṇitākhila-bhramāya ramaṇāya namaḥ

Om! Prostrations to Ramana, who grinds to dust all erroneous perception

२८५ ॐ चैतन्याय रमणाय नमः

285 oṃ caitanyāya ramaṇāya namaḥ

Om! Prostrations to Ramana, who is pure sentience

२८६ ॐ छिन्नग्रन्थिने रमणाय नमः

286 oṃ chinna-granthine ramaṇāya namaḥ

Om! Prostrations to Ramana, who has cut asunder the knot

२८७ ॐ छेदिताखिलबाधकाय रमणाय नमः

287 oṃ cheditākhila-bādhakāya ramaṇāya namaḥ

Om! Prostrations to Ramana, who has cut off all that hinders

२८८ ॐ जगत्प्रियाय रमणाय नमः

288 oṃ jagat-pŕiyāya ramaṇāya namaḥ

Om! Prostrations to Ramana, whom the world loves

२८९ ॐ जगद्गुरवे रमणाय नमः

289 oṃ jagad-gurave ramaṇāya namaḥ

Om! Prostrations to Ramana, the Guru of the world

२९० ॐ जगत्श्रेष्ठाय रमणाय नमः

290 oṃ jagat-śreṣṭhāya ramaṇāya namaḥ

Om! Prostrations to Ramana, the best of all in the world

२९१ ॐ जगत्पतये रमणाय नमः

291 oṃ jagat-pataye ramaṇāya namaḥ

Om! Prostrations to Ramana, the Lord of the world

२९२ ॐ जगत्सेव्याय रमणाय नमः

292 oṃ jagat-sevyāya ramaṇāya namaḥ

Om! Prostrations to Ramana, who should be served by the world

२९३ ॐ जगत्पूज्याय रमणाय नमः

293 oṃ jagat-pūjyāya ramaṇāya namaḥ

Om! Prostrations to Ramana, who should be worshipped by the world

२९४ ॐ जगद्विभवे रमणाय नमः

294 oṃ jagad-vibhave ramaṇāya namaḥ

Om! Prostrations to Ramana, who is the glory of the world

२९५ ॐ जगत्साक्षिणे रमणाय नमः

295 oṃ jagat-sākṣiṇe ramaṇāya namaḥ

Om! Prostrations to Ramana, who is a witness of the world

२९६ ॐ जगदीशाय रमणाय नमः

296 oṃ jagad-īśāya ramaṇāya namaḥ

Om! Prostrations to Ramana, the Lord of the world

२९७ ॐ जगदुद्धारकाय रमणाय नमः

297 oṃ jagad-uddhārakāya ramaṇāya namaḥ

Om! Prostrations to Ramana, the uplifter of the world

२९८ ॐ जगन्मयाय रमणाय नमः

298 oṃ jagan-mayāya ramaṇāya namaḥ

Om! Prostrations to Ramana by whom the world is filled, pervaded

२९९ ॐ जगदानन्दजनकाय रमणाय नमः

299 oṃ jagad-ānanda-janakāya ramaṇāya namaḥ

Om! Prostrations to Ramana, who generates the bliss of the world

३०० ॐ जगद्धिताय रमणाय नमः

300 oṃ jagad-dhitāya ramaṇāya namaḥ

Om! Prostrations to Ramana, who is the welfare of the world

३०१ ॐ जनप्रियाय रमणाय नमः

301 oṃ jana-priyāya ramaṇāya namaḥ

Om! Prostrations to Ramana, who is dear to the people

३०२ ॐ जनाश्रयाय रमणाय नमः

302 oṃ jan-āśrayāya ramaṇāya namaḥ

Om! Prostrations to Ramana, who is the refuge of the people

३०३ ॐ जनजन्मनिबर्हणाय रमणाय नमः

303 oṃ jana-janma-nibarhaṇāya ramaṇāya namaḥ

Om! Prostrations to Ramana, who does away with birth and mundane life

३०४ ॐ जङ्गमाजङ्गमाकाराय रमणाय नमः

304 oṃ jaṅgam-ājaṅgam-ākārāya ramaṇāya namaḥ

Om! Prostrations to Ramana, who is the form of the moving and the unmoving

३०५ ॐ जयापजयपराय रमणाय नमः

305 oṃ jayāpajaya-parāya ramaṇāya namaḥ

Om! Prostrations to Ramana, who is beyond victory and defeat

३०६ ॐ जयिने रमणाय नमः

306 oṃ jayine ramaṇāya namaḥ

Om! Prostrations to Ramana, the victorious

३०७ ॐ जयप्रदाय रमणाय नमः

307 oṃ jaya-pradāya ramaṇāya namaḥ

Om! Prostrations to Ramana, who confers victory

३०८ ॐ जरामरणवर्जिताय रमणाय नमः

308 oṃ jarā-maraṇa-varjitāya ramaṇāya namaḥ

Om! Prostrations to Ramana without senility and death

३०९ ॐ जाग्रते रमणाय नमः

309 oṃ jāgrate ramaṇāya namaḥ

Om! Prostrations to Ramana, who is awake

३१० ॐ जातिमतभेदभञ्जनाय रमणाय नमः

310 oṃ jāti-mata-bheda-bhañjanāya ramaṇāya namaḥ

Om! Prostrations to Ramana, who breaks up the differences of caste and religion

३११ ॐ जितेन्द्रियाय रमणाय नमः

311 oṃ jitendriyāya ramaṇāya namaḥ

Om! Prostrations to Ramana, who has conquered the senses

३१२ ॐ जितकामाय रमणाय नमः

312 oṃ jita-kāmāya ramaṇāya namaḥ

Om! Prostrations to Ramana, who has conquered desire

३१३ ॐ जितक्रोधाय रमणाय नमः

313 oṃ jita-krodhāya ramaṇāya namaḥ

Om! Prostrations to Ramana, who has conquered anger

३१४ ॐ जितलोभाय रमणाय नमः

314 oṃ jita-lobhāya ramaṇāya namaḥ

Om! Prostrations to Ramana, who has conquered greed

३१५ ॐ जितमोहाय रमणाय नमः

315 oṃ jita-mohāya ramaṇāya namaḥ

Om! Prostrations to Ramana, who has conquered delusion

३१६ ॐ जितमदाय रमणाय नमः

316 oṃ jita-madāya ramaṇāya namaḥ

Om! Prostrations to Ramana, who has conquered arrogance

३१७ ॐ जितमात्सर्याय रमणाय नमः

317 oṃ jita-mātsaryāya ramaṇāya namaḥ

Om! Prostrations to Ramana, who has conquered resentment

३१८ ॐ जितामित्राय रमणाय नमः

318 oṃ jit-āmitrāya ramaṇāya namaḥ

Om! Prostrations to Ramana, who has conquered the adversaries

३१९ ॐ जीवाधाराय रमणाय नमः

319 oṃ jīvādhārāya ramaṇāya namaḥ

Om! Prostrations to Ramana, the support of life

३२० ॐ जीवन्मुक्ताय रमणाय नमः

320 oṃ jīvan-muktāya ramaṇāya namaḥ

Om! Prostrations to Ramana liberated while yet in the body

३२१ ॐ जीवब्रह्मैक्यस्वरूपाय रमणाय नमः

321 oṃ jīva-brahmaikya-svarūpāya ramaṇāya namaḥ

Om! Prostrations to Ramana of the nature of the identity of the jiva (individual) and Brahman

३२२ ॐ ज्येष्ठाय रमणाय नमः

322 oṃ jyeṣṭhāya ramaṇāya namaḥ

Om! Prostrations to Ramana, the pre-eminent

३२३ ॐ ज्योतिस्वरूपाय रमणाय नमः

323 oṃ jyoti-svarūpāya ramaṇāya namaḥ

Om! Prostrations to Ramana, of the nature of a flame

३२४ ॐ ज्योतिप्रकाशाय रमणाय नमः

324 oṃ jyoti-prakāśāya ramaṇāya namaḥ

Om! Prostrations to Ramana with the brightness of a flame

३२५ ॐ ज्योतिर्मयाय रमणाय नमः

325 oṃ jyotir-mayāya ramaṇāya namaḥ

Om! Prostrations to Ramana, who is full of light

३२६ ॐ तपःफलाय रमणाय नमः

326 oṃ tapaḥ-phalāya ramaṇāya namaḥ

Om! Prostrations to Ramana, who is the fruit of tapas

३२७ ॐ तपोमयाय रमणाय नमः

327 oṃ tapo-mayāya ramaṇāya namaḥ

Om! Prostrations to Ramana, who is full of tapas

३२८ ॐ तपोवनकृतदेवालयाय रमणाय नमः

328 oṃ tapovana-kṛta-devālayāya ramaṇāya namaḥ

Om! Prostrations to Ramana, who made the temple into a place of tapas

३२९ ॐ तत्पराय रमणाय नमः

329 oṃ tatparāya ramaṇāya namaḥ

Om! Prostrations to Ramana, who is intent on That

३३० ॐ तत्पुरुषाय रमणाय नमः

330 oṃ tat-puruṣāya ramaṇāya namaḥ

Om! Prostrations to Ramana, the person who is That

३३१ ॐ तत्त्वमयाय रमणाय नमः

331 oṃ tattva-mayāya ramaṇāya namaḥ

Om! Prostrations to Ramana, who is full of Truth

३३२ ॐ तत्त्वमस्यादि निरूपणाय रमणाय नमः

332 oṃ tat-tvam-asy-ādi nirūpaṇāya ramaṇāya namaḥ

Om! Prostrations to Ramana, who explains 'That you are' and others (great aphorisms)

३३३ ॐ तत्पदलक्ष्यार्थाय रमणाय नमः

333 oṃ tat-pada-lakṣyārthāya ramaṇāya namaḥ

Om! Prostrations to Ramana, who is the implied meaning of the word 'That'

३३४ ॐ तापत्रयहारिणे रमणाय नमः

334 oṃ tāpa-traya-hāriṇe ramaṇāya namaḥ

Om! Prostrations to Ramana, who takes away the triple afflictions

३३५ ॐ तापत्रयनिर्मुक्ताय रमणाय नमः

335 oṃ tāpa-traya-nirmuktāya ramaṇāya namaḥ

Om! Prostrations to Ramana, who is liberated from the triple afflictions

३३६ ॐ तारकमन्त्राय रमणाय नमः

336 oṃ tāraka-mantrāya ramaṇāya namaḥ

Om! Prostrations to Ramana, who is the mantra for crossing over

३३७ ॐ तारकस्वरूपाय रमणाय नमः

337 oṃ tāraka-svarūpāya ramaṇāya namaḥ

Om! Prostrations to Ramana of the nature of that which carries across

३३८ ॐ तारणाय रमणाय नमः

338 oṃ tāraṇāya ramaṇāya namaḥ

Om! Prostrations to Ramana, who carries across

३३९ ॐ तीक्ष्णबुद्धये रमणाय नमः

339 oṃ tīkṣṇa-buddhaye ramaṇāya namaḥ

Om! Prostrations to Ramana, with a sharp intellect

३४० ॐ तीक्ष्णाय रमणाय नमः

340 oṃ tīkṣṇāya ramaṇāya namaḥ

Om! Prostrations to Ramana, who is sharp

३४१ ॐ तीव्राय रमणाय नमः

341 oṃ tīvrāya ramaṇāya namaḥ

Om! Prostrations to Ramana, who is pervasive

३४२ ॐ तुरीयाय रमणाय नमः

342 oṃ turīyāya ramaṇāya namaḥ

Om! Prostrations to Ramana, who is the fourth state

३४३ ॐ तुरीयातीताय रमणाय नमः

343 oṃ turīyātītāya ramaṇāya namaḥ

Om! Prostrations to Ramana, who transcends the fourth state

३४४ ॐ तुभ्यम् रमणाय नमः

344 oṃ tubhyam ramaṇāya namaḥ

Om! Prostrations to yourself Ramana!

३४५ ॐ तृप्ताय रमणाय नमः

345 oṃ tṛptāya ramaṇāya namaḥ

Om! Prostrations to Ramana, who is contented

३४६ ॐ तेजस्करनिधये रमणाय नमः

346 oṃ tejaskara-nidhaye ramaṇāya namaḥ

Om! Prostrations to Ramana, the treasure granting vital power

३४७ ॐ तेजस्वरूपाय रमणाय नमः

347 oṃ teja-svarūpāya ramaṇāya namaḥ

Om! Prostrations to Ramana of the nature of effulgence

३४८ ॐ तेजसे रमणाय नमः

348 oṃ tejase ramaṇāya namaḥ

Om! Prostrations to Ramana, who is an effulgence

३४९ ॐ तेजोमयाय रमणाय नमः

349 oṃ tejo-mayāya ramaṇāya namaḥ

Om! Prostrations to Ramana filled with effulgence

३५० ॐ त्रिकालदृशे रमणाय नमः

350 oṃ tri-kāla-dṛśe ramaṇāya namaḥ

Om! Prostrations to Ramana, who can see the triple states of time

३५१ ॐ त्रिकालज्ञाय रमणाय नमः

351 oṃ tri-kāla-jñāya ramaṇāya namaḥ

Om! Prostrations to Ramana, who knows all the triple states of time

३५२ ॐ त्रिगुणात्मने रमणाय नमः

352 oṃ tri-guṇ-ātmane ramaṇāya namaḥ

Om! Prostrations to Ramana, who has in him the triple guna-s (qualities)

३५३ ॐ त्रिगुणातीताय रमणाय नमः

353 oṃ tri-guṇ-ātītāya ramaṇāya namaḥ

Om! Prostrations to Ramana, who transcends the triple guna-s (qualities)(sattva, rajas and tamas)

३५४ ॐ त्र्यम्बकाय रमणाय नमः

354 oṃ tryambakāya ramaṇāya namaḥ

Om! Prostrations to Ramana with a triad of eyes

३५५ ॐ त्रयीमयाय रमणाय नमः

355 oṃ trayī-mayāya ramaṇāya namaḥ

Om! Prostrations to Ramana, who pervades the triads

३५६ ॐ त्रिशूलपुरजाताजाताय रमणाय नमः

356 oṃ triśūla-pura-jāt-ājātāya ramaṇāya namaḥ

Om! Prostrations to Ramana, the birthless one who was born in the town of Trisulapura (Tiruchuzhi)

३५७ ॐ दक्षाय रमणाय नमः

357 oṃ dakṣāya ramaṇāya namaḥ

Om! Prostrations to Ramana, who is an expert

३५८ ॐ दक्षिणाभिमुखाय रमणाय नमः

358 oṃ dakṣiṇābhi-mukhāya ramaṇāya namaḥ

Om! Prostrations to Ramana, whose face is turned southwards

३५९ ॐ दक्षिणास्यनिभाननाय रमणाय नमः

359 oṃ dakṣiṇāsya-nibhānanāya ramaṇāya namaḥ

Om! Prostrations to Ramana, who shines with a south-turned head

३६० ॐ दक्षिणामूर्तिस्वरूपाय रमणाय नमः

360 oṃ dakṣiṇāmūrti-svarūpāya ramaṇāya namaḥ

Om! Prostrations to Ramana, who is of the nature of Dakshinamurti

३६१ ॐ दक्षिणादक्षिणाराध्याय रमणाय नमः

361 oṃ dakṣiṇ-ādakṣiṇ-ārādhyāya ramaṇāya namaḥ

Om! Prostrations to Ramana, who is to be worshipped by both the intelligent and simple-minded

३६२ ॐ दक्षिणामूर्तिसंदर्शकाय रमणाय नमः

362 oṃ dakṣiṇāmūrti-saṃdarśakāya ramaṇāya namaḥ

Om! Prostrations to Ramana, who reveals Dakshinamurti

३६३ ॐ दण्डपाणये रमणाय नमः

363 oṃ daṇḍa-pāṇaye ramaṇāya namaḥ

Om! Prostrations to Ramana, who holds a staff in the hand

३६४ ॐ दत्तात्रेयाय रमणाय नमः

364 oṃ dattātreyāya ramaṇāya namaḥ

Om! Prostrations to Ramana, the incarnation of Datta, son of Arti (Dattatreya)

३६५ ॐ दयामूर्तये रमणाय नमः

365 oṃ dayā-mūrtaye ramaṇāya namaḥ

Om! Prostrations to Ramana, the embodiment of sympathy

३६६ ॐ दयानिधये रमणाय नमः

366 oṃ dayā-nidhaye ramaṇāya namaḥ

Om! Prostrations to Ramana, the treasure of sympathy

३६७ ॐ दयार्णवाय रमणाय नमः

367 oṃ dayārṇavāya ramaṇāya namaḥ

Om! Prostrations to Ramana, the ocean of sympathy

३६८ ॐ दर्शनीयाय रमणाय नमः

368 oṃ darśanīyāya ramaṇāya namaḥ

Om! Prostrations to Ramana, who is good to look at

३६९ ॐ दर्शनादघसंहारिणे रमणाय नमः

369 oṃ darśanād-agha-saṃhāriṇe ramaṇāya namaḥ

Om! Prostrations to Ramana, who destroys sin by a look

३७० ॐ दहराकाशस्वरूपिणे रमणाय नमः

370 oṃ dahar-ākāśa-svarūpiṇe ramaṇāya namaḥ

Om! Prostrations to Ramana of the nature of the heart-space

३७१ ॐ दानप्रियाय रमणाय नमः

371 oṃ dāna-priyāya ramaṇāya namaḥ

Om! Prostrations to Ramana, who likes to give gifts

३७२ ॐ स्वदानपरदानाभेदाय रमणाय नमः

372 oṃ sva-dāna-paradān-ābhedāya ramaṇāya namaḥ

Om! Prostrations to Ramana, who does not distinguish between gift to oneself and gift to others

३७३ ॐ दानशूराय रमणाय नमः

373 oṃ dāna-śūrāya ramaṇāya namaḥ

Om! Prostrations to Ramana, who is a hero in being charitable

३७४ ॐ दान्ताय रमणाय नमः

374 oṃ dāntāya ramaṇāya namaḥ

Om! Prostrations to Ramana with fortitude

३७५ ॐ दिगम्बराय रमणाय नमः

375 oṃ dig-ambarāya ramaṇāya namaḥ

Om! Prostrations to Ramana with the directions as his vestment, without garments

३७६ ॐ दिव्याय रमणाय नमः

376 oṃ divyāya ramaṇāya namaḥ

Om! Prostrations to Ramana, the shining

३७७ ॐ दिव्यसुन्दराय रमणाय नमः

377 oṃ divya-sundarāya ramaṇāya namaḥ

Om! Prostrations to Ramana divinely beautiful

३७८ ॐ दिव्यज्ञाय रमणाय नमः

378 oṃ divya-jñāya ramaṇāya namaḥ

Om! Prostrations to Ramana having knowledge of the divine

३७९ ॐ दीक्षिताय रमणाय नमः

379 oṃ dīkṣitāya ramaṇāya namaḥ

Om! Prostrations to Ramana, one who has consecrated oneself

३८० ॐ दीनजनसहायाय रमणाय नमः

380 oṃ dīna-jana-sahāyāya ramaṇāya namaḥ

Om! Prostrations to Ramana, who is the helper of the depressed

३८१ ॐ दीनजनबन्धवे रमणाय नमः

381 oṃ dīna-jana-bandhave ramaṇāya namaḥ

Om! Prostrations to Ramana, who is a friend of the depressed

३८२ ॐ दीनजनपोषणाय रमणाय नमः

382 oṃ dīna-jana-poṣaṇāya ramaṇāya namaḥ

Om! Prostrations to Ramana, who nourishes the depressed

३८३ ॐ दीनदयालवे रमणाय नमः

383 oṃ dīna-dayālave ramaṇāya namaḥ

Om! Prostrations to Ramana, who has sympathy for the depressed

३८४ ॐ दीनसंतापनाशनाय रमणाय नमः

384 oṃ dīna-saṃtāpa-nāśanāya ramaṇāya namaḥ

Om! Prostrations to Ramana, who destroys the anguish of the depressed

३८५ ॐ दीनोद्धारकाय रमणाय नमः

385 oṃ dīnoddhārakāya ramaṇāya namaḥ

Om! Prostrations to Ramana, the uplifter of the depressed

३८६ ॐ दीप्ताय रमणाय नमः

386 oṃ dīptāya ramaṇāya namaḥ

Om! Prostrations to Ramana, who is brilliant

३८७ ॐ दीर्घाय रमणाय नमः

387 oṃ dīrghāya ramaṇāya namaḥ

Om! Prostrations to Ramana, who is lofty

३८८ ॐ दीर्घव्रताय रमणाय नमः

388 oṃ dīrgha-vratāya ramaṇāya namaḥ

Om! Prostrations to Ramana, who has a long-lasting vow

३८९ ॐ दीर्घदर्शनाय रमणाय नमः

389 oṃ dīrgha-darśanāya ramaṇāya namaḥ

Om! Prostrations to Ramana, who has great foresight

३९० ॐ दुःखनिवारणाय रमणाय नमः

390 oṃ duḥkha-nivāraṇāya ramaṇāya namaḥ

Om! Prostrations to Ramana, who wards off sorrow

३९१ ॐ दुष्टाहंकारनाशनाय रमणाय नमः

391 oṃ duṣṭ-āhaṃkāra-nāśanāya ramaṇāya namaḥ

Om! Prostrations to Ramana, who destroys the troublesome ego

३९२ ॐ दृग्दृश्यविवेकाय रमणाय नमः

392 oṃ dṛg-dṛśya-vivekāya ramaṇāya namaḥ

Om! Prostrations to Ramana with the discrimination between the seer and the seen

३९३ ॐ दृढनिश्चयाय रमणाय नमः

393 oṃ dṛḍha-niścayāya ramaṇāya namaḥ

Om! Prostrations to Ramana with a steadfast certitude

३९४ ॐ दृढाय रमणाय नमः

394 oṃ dṛḍhāya ramaṇāya namaḥ

Om! Prostrations to Ramana, who is steadfastness himself

३९५ ॐ दृश्यरहिताय रमणाय नमः

395 oṃ dṛśya-rahitāya ramaṇāya namaḥ

Om! Prostrations to Ramana, who has nothing to see

३९६ ॐ देवाय रमणाय नमः

396 oṃ devāya ramaṇāya namaḥ

Om! Prostrations to Ramana, the god, the divine

३९७ ॐ देवतमाय रमणाय नमः

397 oṃ deva-tamāya ramaṇāya namaḥ

Om! Prostrations to Ramana, the best of the gods

३९८ ॐ देवदेवाय रमणाय नमः

398 oṃ deva-devāya ramaṇāya namaḥ

Om! Prostrations to Ramana, the god of the gods

३९९ ॐ देवीकालोत्तरदेशिकाय रमणाय नमः

399 oṃ devī-kālottara-deśikāya ramaṇāya namaḥ

Om! Prostrations to Ramana, the master showing the way to Devikalottara

४०० ॐ दैन्यहारिणे रमणाय नमः

400 oṃ dainya-hāriṇe ramaṇāya namaḥ

Om! Prostrations to Ramana, who takes away depression

४०१ ॐ दोषवर्जिताय रमणाय नमः

401 oṃ doṣa-varjitāya ramaṇāya namaḥ

Om! Prostrations to Ramana, who is without faults

४०२ ॐ दोषनिवारिणे रमणाय नमः

402 oṃ doṣa-nivāriṇe ramaṇāya namaḥ

Om! Prostrations to Ramana, who prevents faults

४०३ ॐ द्वन्द्वदुःखहरणाय रमणाय नमः

403 oṃ dvandva-duḥkha-haraṇāya ramaṇāya namaḥ

Om! Prostrations to Ramana, who removes the pain of the pairs of opposites

४०४ ॐ द्वन्द्वातीताय रमणाय नमः

404 oṃ dvandvātītāya ramaṇāya namaḥ

Om! Prostrations to Ramana, who transcends pairs of opposites

४०५ ॐ धन्याय रमणाय नमः

405 oṃ dhanyāya ramaṇāya namaḥ

Om! Prostrations to Ramana, who is blessed

४०६ ॐ धर्मिष्ठाय रमणाय नमः

406 oṃ dharmiṣṭāya ramaṇāya namaḥ

Om! Prostrations to Ramana, who is of righteous conduct

४०७ ॐ धर्मकृते रमणाय नमः

407 oṃ dharma-kṛte ramaṇāya namaḥ

Om! Prostrations to Ramana, who does virtuous acts

४०८ ॐ धर्मचारिणे रमणाय नमः

408 oṃ dharma-cāriṇe ramaṇāya namaḥ

Om! Prostrations to Ramana, who treads the path of righteousness

४०९ ॐ धर्मतत्पराय रमणाय नमः

409 oṃ dharma-tatparāya ramaṇāya namaḥ

Om! Prostrations to Ramana, whose goal is the natural law

४१० ॐ धर्मपोषकाय रमणाय नमः

410 oṃ dharma-poṣakāya ramaṇāya namaḥ

Om! Prostrations to Ramana, who nurtures righteousness

४११ ॐ धर्मातीताय रमणाय नमः

411 oṃ dharmātītāya ramaṇāya namaḥ

Om! Prostrations to Ramana, who transcends the laws of conduct

४१२ ॐ धात्रे रमणाय नमः

412 oṃ dhātre ramaṇāya namaḥ

Om! Prostrations to Ramana, who is the support

४१३ ॐ धीराय रमणाय नमः

413 oṃ dhīrāya ramaṇāya namaḥ

Om! Prostrations to Ramana, the valorous

४१४ ॐ धीरोदात्ताय रमणाय नमः

414 oṃ dhīrodāttāya ramaṇāya namaḥ

Om! Prostrations to Ramana, the highly valorous

४१५ ॐ धूमकेतनाय रमणाय नमः

415 oṃ dhūma-ketanāya ramaṇāya namaḥ

Om! Prostrations to Ramana, who has the banner of smoke, fire

४१६ ॐ धृतिमते रमणाय नमः

416 oṃ dhṛtimate ramaṇāya namaḥ

Om! Prostrations to Ramana of steadfast mind

४१७ ॐ धृतये रमणाय नमः

417 oṃ dhṛtaye ramaṇāya namaḥ

Om! Prostrations to Ramana, who is firmness itself

४१८ ॐ ध्रुवाय रमणाय नमः

418 oṃ dhruvāya ramaṇāya namaḥ

Om! Prostrations to Ramana, the fixed, one who is the fixed celestial pole star

४१९ ॐ नन्दनाय रमणाय नमः

419 oṃ nandanāya ramaṇāya namaḥ

Om! Prostrations to Ramana, who gives joy

४२० ॐ नमिताशेषदुःखहृदे रमणाय नमः

420 oṃ namit-āśeṣa-duḥkha-hṛde ramaṇāya namaḥ

Om! Prostrations to Ramana, the remover of sorrow of the endless who bow to him

४२१ ॐ नरकविनाशनाय रमणाय नमः

421 oṃ naraka-vināśanāya ramaṇāya namaḥ

Om! Prostrations to Ramana, who destroys hell

४२२ ॐ नरर्षभाय रमणाय नमः

422 oṃ nararṣabhāya ramaṇāya namaḥ

Om! Prostrations to Ramana, the mighty (bull) among men

४२३ ॐ निगमातीताय रमणाय नमः

423 oṃ nigam-ātītāya ramaṇāya namaḥ

Om! Prostrations to Ramana, who transcends the Veda-s

४२४ ॐ निमित्ताय रमणाय नमः

424 oṃ nimittāya ramaṇāya namaḥ

Om! Prostrations to Ramana, who is the instrumental cause

४२५ ॐ नियमस्वभावाय रमणाय नमः

425 oṃ niyama-svabhāvāya ramaṇāya namaḥ

Om! Prostrations to Ramana, who is disciplined naturally

४२६ ॐ नित्याय रमणाय नमः

426 oṃ nityāya ramaṇāya namaḥ

Om! Prostrations to Ramana, who is eternal

४२७ ॐ नित्यक्लिन्नाय रमणाय नमः

427 oṃ nitya-klinnāya ramaṇāya namaḥ

Om! Prostrations to Ramana, who is ever moist with compassion

४२८ ॐ नित्यपूजास्मरणाय रमणाय नमः

428 oṃ nitya-pūjā-smaraṇāya ramaṇāya namaḥ

Om! Prostrations to Ramana, who is daily thought of in prayer, worship

४२९ ॐ नित्यमुक्ताय रमणाय नमः

429 oṃ nitya-muktāya ramaṇāya namaḥ

Om! Prostrations to Ramana, who is ever liberated

४३० ॐ नित्यबुद्धाय रमणाय नमः

430 oṃ nitya-buddhāya ramaṇāya namaḥ

Om! Prostrations to Ramana, who is ever awake, intelligent

४३१ ॐ नित्यशुद्धाय रमणाय नमः

431 oṃ nitya-śuddhāya ramaṇāya namaḥ

Om! Prostrations to Ramana, who is ever pure

४३२ ॐ नित्यानन्दाय रमणाय नमः

432 oṃ nity-ānandāya ramaṇāya namaḥ

Om! Prostrations to Ramana, who is ever in bliss

४३३ ॐ नित्यपुरुषाय रमणाय नमः

433 oṃ nitya-puruṣāya ramaṇāya namaḥ

Om! Prostrations to Ramana, the eternal spirit

४३४ ॐ नित्योत्सवाय रमणाय नमः

434 oṃ nityo-tsavāya ramaṇāya namaḥ

Om! Prostrations to Ramana, who is always in festivity

४३५ ॐ नित्यवैभवाय रमणाय नमः

435 oṃ nitya-vaibhavāya ramaṇāya namaḥ

Om! Prostrations to Ramana, who is ever in glory

४३६ ॐ नित्यरमणाय रमणाय नमः

436 oṃ nitya-ramaṇāya ramaṇāya namaḥ

Om! Prostrations to Ramana, who is ever enjoying

४३७ ॐ निर्विकाराय रमणाय नमः

437 oṃ nir-vikārāya ramaṇāya namaḥ

Om! Prostrations to Ramana, who is unchanged

४३८ ॐ निर्गुणाय रमणाय नमः

438 oṃ nir-guṇāya ramaṇāya namaḥ

Om! Prostrations to Ramana without qualities

४३९ ॐ निरञ्जनाय रमणाय नमः

439 oṃ nir-añjanāya ramaṇāya namaḥ

Om! Prostrations to Ramana, the taintless

४४० ॐ निरुपाधिने रमणाय नमः

440 oṃ nir-upādhine ramaṇāya namaḥ

Om! Prostrations to Ramana without limitations

४४१ ॐ निर्ममाय रमणाय नमः

441 oṃ nir-mamāya ramaṇāya namaḥ

Om! Prostrations to Ramana, who has no 'my-ness'

४४२ ॐ निरहंकाराय रमणाय नमः

442 oṃ nir-ahaṃkārāya ramaṇāya namaḥ

Om! Prostrations to Ramana, the egoless

४४३ ॐ निर्लेपाय रमणाय नमः

443 oṃ nir-lepāya ramaṇāya namaḥ

Om! Prostrations to Ramana, who is unsmeared, taintless

४४४ ॐ निर्मोहाय रमणाय नमः

444 oṃ nir-mohāya ramaṇāya namaḥ

Om! Prostrations to Ramana without delusion

४४५ ॐ निर्मदाय रमणाय नमः

445 oṃ nir-madāya ramaṇāya namaḥ

Om! Prostrations to Ramana without arrogance

४४६ ॐ निरवग्रहाय रमणाय नमः

446 oṃ nir-avagrahāya ramaṇāya namaḥ

Om! Prostrations to Ramana, who is without any impediment, restraint

४४७ ॐ निरुपमाय रमणाय नमः

447 oṃ nir-upamāya ramaṇāya namaḥ

Om! Prostrations to Ramana, the incomparable

४४८ ॐ निर्मलाय रमणाय नमः

448 oṃ nir-malāya ramaṇāya namaḥ

Om! Prostrations to Ramana, the blemishless

४४९ ॐ निराश्रयाय रमणाय नमः

449 oṃ nir-āśrayāya ramaṇāya namaḥ

Om! Prostrations to Ramana, who needs no support

४५० ॐ निरालम्बाय नमः

450 oṃ nir-ālambāya namaḥ

Om! Prostrations to Ramana, who needs nothing upon which to depend

४५१ ॐ निराकुलाय रमणाय नमः

451 oṃ nir-ākulāya ramaṇāya namaḥ

Om! Prostrations to Ramana without confusion, perplexity

४५२ ॐ निरामयाय रमणाय नमः

452 oṃ nir-āmayāya ramaṇāya namaḥ

Om! Prostrations to Ramana without affliction

४५३ ॐ निराबाधाय रमणाय नमः

453 oṃ nir-ābādhāya ramaṇāya namaḥ

Om! Prostrations to Ramana, who is undisturbed

४५४ ॐ निरातङ्काय रमणाय नमः

454 oṃ nir-ātaṅkāya ramaṇāya namaḥ

Om! Prostrations to Ramana without the sickness of the body or mind, without fatigue, without afflictions of mind

४५५ ॐ निर्जराय रमणाय नमः

455 oṃ nir-jarāya ramaṇāya namaḥ

Om! Prostrations to Ramana, who is un-aging

४५६ ॐ निरत्ययाय रमणाय नमः

456 oṃ nir-atyayāya ramaṇāya namaḥ

Om! Prostrations to Ramana, who is infallible

४५७ ॐ निर्भवाय रमणाय नमः

457 oṃ nir-bhavāya ramaṇāya namaḥ

Om! Prostrations to Ramana, who is unborn, has no worldly existence

४५८ ॐ निर्भयाय रमणाय नमः

458 oṃ nir-bhayāya ramaṇāya namaḥ

Om! Prostrations to Ramana, the fearless

४५९ ॐ निर्भेदाय रमणाय नमः

459 oṃ nir-bhedāya ramaṇāya namaḥ

Om! Prostrations to Ramana, the difference-less

४६० ॐ निर्विकाराय रमणाय नमः

460 oṃ nir-vikārāya ramaṇāya namaḥ

Om! Prostrations to Ramana without modifications

४६१ ॐ निर्नाशाय रमणाय नमः

461 oṃ nir-nāśāya ramaṇāya namaḥ

Om! Prostrations to Ramana, the destruction-less

४६२ ॐ निर्विकल्पाय रमणाय नमः

462 oṃ nir-vikalpāya ramaṇāya namaḥ

Om! Prostrations to Ramana without erroneous ideas

४६३ ॐ निर्लोभाय रमणाय नमः

463 oṃ nir-lobhāya ramaṇāya namaḥ

Om! Prostrations to Ramana without covetousness

४६४ ॐ निराधाराय रमणाय नमः

464 oṃ nir-ādhārāya ramaṇāya namaḥ

Om! Prostrations to Ramana, who is without support

४६५ ॐ निरपायाय रमणाय नमः

465 oṃ nir-apāyāya ramaṇāya namaḥ

Om! Prostrations to Ramana, who is imperishable

४६६ ॐ निर्वाणसुखदाय रमणाय नमः

466 oṃ nirvāṇa-sukha-dāya ramaṇāya namaḥ

Om! Prostrations to Ramana, who gives the bliss of liberation

४६७ ॐ निवृत्तये रमणाय नमः

467 oṃ nivṛttaye ramaṇāya namaḥ

Om! Prostrations to Ramana, who turns inward

४६८ ॐ निश्चलाय रमणाय नमः

468 oṃ niś-calāya ramaṇāya namaḥ

Om! Prostrations to Ramana without movement

४६९ ॐ निश्चलतत्त्वाय रमणाय नमः

469 oṃ niścala-tattvāya ramaṇāya namaḥ

Om! Prostrations to Ramana, who is the truth of changelessness

४७० ॐ निश्चलात्मने रमणाय नमः

470 oṃ niścal-ātmane ramaṇāya namaḥ

Om! Prostrations to Ramana, who is possessed of changelessness

४७१ ॐ निश्चिन्ताय रमणाय नमः

471 oṃ niś-cintāya ramaṇāya namaḥ

Om! Prostrations to Ramana without thoughts

४७२ ॐ निष्फलाय रमणाय नमः

472 oṃ niṣ-phalāya ramaṇāya namaḥ

Om! Prostrations to Ramana, who is without any [thought of] fruits, results

४७३ ॐ निष्कलङ्काय रमणाय नमः

473 oṃ niṣ-kalaṅkāya ramaṇāya namaḥ

Om! Prostrations to Ramana, who is without blemish

४७४ ॐ निष्कामाय रमणाय नमः

474 oṃ niṣ-kāmāya ramaṇāya namaḥ

Om! Prostrations to Ramana, who is without desire

४७५ ॐ निष्क्रोधाय रमणाय नमः

475 oṃ niṣ-krodhāya ramaṇāya namaḥ

Om! Prostrations to Ramana, who is without anger

४७६ ॐ निष्कारणाय रमणाय नमः

476 oṃ niṣ-kāraṇāya ramaṇāya namaḥ

Om! Prostrations to Ramana, the causeless

४७७ ॐ निष्क्रियाय रमणाय नमः

477 oṃ niṣ-kriyāya ramaṇāya namaḥ

Om! Prostrations to Ramana, the action-less

४७८ ॐ निष्परिग्रहाय रमणाय नमः

478 oṃ niṣ-parigrahāya ramaṇāya namaḥ

Om! Prostrations to Ramana, the possessionless

४७९ ॐ निष्पापाय रमणाय नमः

479 oṃ niṣ-pāpāya ramaṇāya namaḥ

Om! Prostrations to Ramana, who is sinless

४८० ॐ निष्प्रपञ्चाय रमणाय नमः

480 oṃ niṣ-prapañcāya ramaṇāya namaḥ

Om! Prostrations to Ramana without the manifest world

४८१ ॐ निस्सङ्गाय रमणाय नमः

481 oṃ nis-saṅgāya ramaṇāya namaḥ

Om! Prostrations to Ramana, who is without attachments, without association

४८२ ॐ निस्तुलाय रमणाय नमः

482 oṃ nis-tulāya ramaṇāya namaḥ

Om! Prostrations to Ramana, who is without comparison

४८३ ॐ निस्संशयाय रमणाय नमः

483 oṃ nis-saṃśayāya ramaṇāya namaḥ

Om! Prostrations to Ramana, who has no doubts

४८४ ॐ निस्त्रैगुण्याय रमणाय नमः

484 oṃ nis-traiguṇyāya ramaṇāya namaḥ

Om! Prostrations to Ramana, who is without the triad of qualities

४८५ ॐ नीतये रमणाय नमः

485 oṃ nītaye ramaṇāya namaḥ

Om! Prostrations to Ramana, who leads

४८६ ॐ नीरागाय रमणाय नमः

486 oṃ nī-rāgāya ramaṇāya namaḥ

Om! Prostrations to Ramana, the attachmentless, the passionless

४८७ ॐ नैकसानुचराय रमणाय नमः

487 oṃ naika-sānucarāya ramaṇāya namaḥ

Om! Prostrations to Ramana, who has many followers with him

४८८ ॐ न्यग्रोधमूलवासिने रमणाय नमः

488 oṃ nyagrodha-mūla-vāsine ramaṇāya namaḥ

Om! Prostrations to Ramana, who resides at the foot of the banyan tree

४८९ ॐ पण्डिताय रमणाय नमः

489 oṃ paṇḍitāya ramaṇāya namaḥ

Om! Prostrations to Ramana, the learned one

४९० ॐ पतितपावनाय रमणाय नमः

490 oṃ patita-pāvanāya ramaṇāya namaḥ

Om! Prostrations to Ramana, who purifies the fallen

४९१ ॐ पञ्चकोशातीताय रमणाय नमः

491 oṃ pañca-kośātītāya ramaṇāya namaḥ

Om! Prostrations to Ramana, who transcends the pentad of sheaths

४९२ ॐ पञ्चवक्त्राय रमणाय नमः

492 oṃ pañca-vaktrāya ramaṇāya namaḥ

Om! Prostrations to Ramana having five faces

४९३ ॐ पराय रमणाय नमः

493 oṃ parāya ramaṇāya namaḥ

Om! Prostrations to Ramana, the Supreme

४९४ ॐ परात्पराय रमणाय नमः

494 oṃ parāt-parāya ramaṇāya namaḥ

Om! Prostrations to Ramana, who is beyond the Supreme

४९५ ॐ परमेश्वराय रमणाय नमः

495 oṃ parameśvarāya ramaṇāya namaḥ

Om! Prostrations to Ramana, the Supreme Lord

४९६ ॐ परमपवित्राय रमणाय नमः

496 oṃ parama-pavitrāya ramaṇāya namaḥ

Om! Prostrations to Ramana, the supremely holy

४९७ ॐ परमानन्दमूर्तये रमणाय नमः

497 oṃ paramānanda-mūrtaye ramaṇāya namaḥ

Om! Prostrations to Ramana, who is of the nature of supreme bliss

४९८ ॐ परमाचार्याय रमणाय नमः

498 oṃ param-ācāryāya ramaṇāya namaḥ

Om! Prostrations to Ramana, the Supreme Master

४९९ ॐ परमार्थविदे रमणाय नमः

499 oṃ paramārtha-vide ramaṇāya namaḥ

Om! Prostrations to Ramana, who knows the highest Truth

५०० ॐ परस्मै ज्योतिषे रमणाय नमः

500 oṃ parasmai jyotiṣe ramaṇāya namaḥ

Om! Prostrations to Ramana, the Supreme Light

५०१ ॐ परस्मै प्रकाशाय रमणाय नमः

501 oṃ parasmai prakāśāya ramaṇāya namaḥ

Om! Prostrations to Ramana, the supremely shining

५०२ ॐ परस्मै हिताय रमणाय नमः

502 oṃ parasmai hitāya ramaṇāya namaḥ

Om! Prostrations to Ramana, the supremely beneficial

५०३ ॐ परिपालकाय रमणाय नमः

503 oṃ paripālakāya ramaṇāya namaḥ

Om! Prostrations to Ramana, the ruler

५०४ ॐ परमानन्ददाय रमणाय नमः

504 oṃ paramānanda-dāya ramaṇāya namaḥ

Om! Prostrations to Ramana, who gives supreme bliss

५०५ ॐ परोपकारतत्पराय रमणाय नमः

505 oṃ paropakāra-tatparāya ramaṇāya namaḥ

Om! Prostrations to Ramana, who is intent on helping others

५०६ ॐ पराशरकुलोत्तंसाय रमणाय नमः

506 oṃ parāśara-kulottaṃsāya ramaṇāya namaḥ

Om! Prostrations to Ramana born in the lineage of sage Parasara

५०७ ॐ पाकशास्त्रपारङ्गताय रमणाय नमः

507 oṃ pāka-śāstra-pāraṅgatāya ramaṇāya namaḥ

Om! Prostrations to Ramana, the pastmaster in the science of cooking

५०८ ॐ पाककलानिपुणाय रमणाय नमः

508 oṃ pāka-kalā-nipuṇāya ramaṇāya namaḥ

Om! Prostrations to Ramana, the expert in the art of cooking

५०९ ॐ परिपक्वज्ञानपरिचारकाय रमणाय नमः

509 oṃ paripakva-jñāna-paricārakāya ramaṇāya namaḥ

Om! Prostrations to Ramana, who serves well-cooked Knowledge

५१० ॐ पावकात्मजाय रमणाय नमः

510 oṃ pāvakātmajāya ramaṇāya namaḥ

Om! Prostrations to Ramana, the son of the god of fire

५११ ॐ पापनाशिने रमणाय नमः

511 oṃ pāpanāśine ramaṇāya namaḥ

Om! Prostrations to Ramana, the destroyer of sin (demerit)

५१२ ॐ पावनाय रमणाय नमः

512 oṃ pāvanāya ramaṇāya namaḥ

Om! Prostrations to Ramana, the holy one

५१३ ॐ पापविदूराय रमणाय नमः

513 oṃ pāpa-vidūrāya ramaṇāya namaḥ

Om! Prostrations to Ramana, who drives afar sin (demerit)

५१४ ॐ पावकोज्ज्वलाय रमणाय नमः

514 oṃ pāvakojjvalāya ramaṇāya namaḥ

Om! Prostrations to Ramana, who glows like fire

५१५ ॐ पावनचरित्राय रमणाय नमः

515 oṃ pāvana-caritrāya ramaṇāya namaḥ

Om! Prostrations to Ramana, who has a holy history

५१६ ॐ पितृपदान्वेषिणे रमणाय नमः

516 oṃ pitṛ-padānveṣiṇe ramaṇāya namaḥ

Om! Prostrations to Ramana in search of the feet of his Father

५१७ ॐ पुण्यवचसे रमणाय नमः

517 oṃ puṇya-vacase ramaṇāya namaḥ

Om! Prostrations to Ramana of holy words

५१८ ॐ पुण्यकृते रमणाय नमः

518 oṃ puṇya-kṛte ramaṇāya namaḥ

Om! Prostrations to Ramana of holy acts

५१९ ॐ पुण्यपुरुषाय रमणाय नमः

519 oṃ puṇya-puruṣāya ramaṇāya namaḥ

Om! Prostrations to Ramana, the holy man

५२० ॐ पुण्यश्रवणकीर्तनाय रमणाय नमः

520 oṃ puṇya-śravaṇa-kīrtanāya ramaṇāya namaḥ

Om! Prostrations to Ramana, whose fame it is holy to hear

५२१ ॐ पुण्याय रमणाय नमः

521 oṃ puṇyāya ramaṇāya namaḥ

Om! Prostrations to Ramana, who is himself holiness, good merit

५२२ ॐ पुराणपुरुषाय रमणाय नमः

522 oṃ purāṇa-puruṣāya ramaṇāya namaḥ

Om! Prostrations to Ramana, the person of the puranas, worthy of the purana-s

५२३ ॐ पुरातनाय रमणाय नमः

523 oṃ purātanāya ramaṇāya namaḥ

Om! Prostrations to Ramana, the ancient one

५२४ ॐ पुष्टये नमः

524 oṃ puṣṭaye namaḥ

Om! Prostrations to Ramana, who is himself nourishment

५२५ ॐ पुरोगमाय रमणाय नमः

525 oṃ purogamāya ramaṇāya namaḥ

Om! Prostrations to Ramana, who goes in front

५२६ ॐ पुरुषोत्तमाय रमणाय नमः

526 oṃ puruṣottamāya ramaṇāya namaḥ

Om! Prostrations to Ramana, the best among men

५२७ ॐ पूज्याय रमणाय नमः

527 oṃ pūjyāya ramaṇāya namaḥ

Om! Prostrations to Ramana, who is fit to be worshipped

५२८ ॐ पूर्णबोधाय रमणाय नमः

528 oṃ pūrṇa-bodhāya ramaṇāya namaḥ

Om! Prostrations to Ramana with perfect, complete, knowledge

५२९ ॐ पूर्णानन्दाय रमणाय नमः

529 oṃ pūrṇānandāya ramaṇāya namaḥ

Om! Prostrations to Ramana, who is in perfect bliss

५३० ॐ पूर्णाय रमणाय नमः

530 oṃ pūrṇāya ramaṇāya namaḥ

Om! Prostrations to Ramana, who is perfect

५३१ ॐ पुष्कराय रमणाय नमः

531 oṃ puṣkarāya ramaṇāya namaḥ

Om! Prostrations to Ramana, the Sun

५३२ ॐ प्रग्रहाय रमणाय नमः

532 oṃ pragrahāya ramaṇāya namaḥ

Om! Prostrations to Ramana, who befriends

५३३ ॐ प्रकृतिनिराकृताय रमणाय नमः

533 oṃ prakṛti-nirākṛtāya ramaṇāya namaḥ

Om! Prostrations to Ramana, who rejects prakrti (manifestation)

५३४ ॐ प्रधानाय रमणाय नमः

534 oṃ pradhānāya ramaṇāya namaḥ

Om! Prostrations to Ramana, who is the most important

५३५ ॐ प्रकाशाय रमणाय नमः

535 oṃ prakāśāya ramaṇāya namaḥ

Om! Prostrations to Ramana, the luminous

५३६ ॐ प्रकाशात्मने रमणाय नमः

536 oṃ prakāśātmane ramaṇāya namaḥ

Om! Prostrations to Ramana, the shining Self

५३७ ॐ प्रशान्ताय रमणाय नमः

537 oṃ praśāntāya ramaṇāya namaḥ

Om! Prostrations to Ramana, the intensely peaceful

५३८ ॐ प्रशान्तात्मने रमणाय नमः

538 oṃ praśānt-ātmane ramaṇāya namaḥ

Om! Prostrations to Ramana, who has intense peace in himself, the intensely peaceful Self

५३९ ॐ प्रज्ञानाय रमणाय नमः

539 oṃ prajñānāya ramaṇāya namaḥ

Om! Prostrations to Ramana, who is himself exalted Knowledge

५४० ॐ प्रियाय रमणाय नमः

540 oṃ priyāya ramaṇāya namaḥ

Om! Prostrations to Ramana, the beloved one

५४१ ॐ प्रियदर्शनाय रमणाय नमः

541 oṃ priya-darśanāya ramaṇāya namaḥ

Om! Prostrations to Ramana, who is lovable to look at

५४२ ॐ प्रीतिविवर्धनाय रमणाय नमः

542 oṃ prīti-vivardhanāya ramaṇāya namaḥ

Om! Prostrations to Ramana, who nourishes, enhances, love

५४३ ॐ प्रेमस्वरूपाय रमणाय नमः

543 oṃ prema-svarūpāya ramaṇāya namaḥ

Om! Prostrations to Ramana, who is of the nature of love

५४४ ॐ प्रेमात्मने रमणाय नमः

544 oṃ premātmane ramaṇāya namaḥ

Om! Prostrations to Ramana, who has love in himself, the Self of love

५४५ ॐ प्रणतार्तिहराय रमणाय नमः

545 oṃ praṇat-ārti-harāya ramaṇāya namaḥ

Om! Prostrations to Ramana, who relieves the distress of those who bow

५४६ ॐ प्रपन्नार्तिहराय रमणाय नमः

546 oṃ prapann-ārti-harāya ramaṇāya namaḥ

Om! Prostrations to Ramana, who takes away the distress of a supplicant

५४७ ॐ प्रत्यगात्मने रमणाय नमः

547 oṃ pratyag-ātmane ramaṇāya namaḥ

Om! Prostrations to Ramana, the Self in everything

५४८ ॐ प्रत्यग्भूतवासाय रमणाय नमः

548 oṃ pratyag-bhūta-vāsāya ramaṇāya namaḥ

Om! Prostrations to Ramana, who dwells in every individual being

५४९ ॐ प्रत्याय रमणाय नमः

549 oṃ pratyāya ramaṇāya namaḥ

Om! Prostrations to Ramana, who is the proof

५५० ॐ प्रत्यक्षात्मने रमणाय नमः

550 oṃ pratyakṣātmane ramaṇāya namaḥ

Om! Prostrations to Ramana, the Self that is in one's direct presence

५५१ ॐ प्रवृत्तये रमणाय नमः

551 oṃ pravṛttaye ramaṇāya namaḥ

Om! Prostrations to Ramana, who goes forward

५५२ ॐ प्रणवभूताय रमणाय नमः

552 oṃ praṇava-bhūtāya ramaṇāya namaḥ

Om! Prostrations to Ramana, who exists as Pranava (Om)

५५३ ॐ प्रणवस्वरूपाय रमणाय नमः

553 oṃ praṇava-svarūpāya ramaṇāya namaḥ

Om! Prostrations to Ramana, who is of the nature of Pranava (Om)

५५४ ॐ प्रमाथिवर्षधनुर्मासपुनर्वसुनक्षत्रजन्मने रमणाय नमः

554 oṃ pramāthi-varṣa-dhanur-māsa-punar-vasu-nakṣatra-janmane ramaṇāya namaḥ

Om! Prostrations to Ramana, whose birth [on earth] was in the year Pramathi in the month of Dhanus in the asterism Punarvasu

५५५ ॐ फुल्लाम्बुजलोचनाय रमणाय नमः

555 oṃ phullāmbuja-locanāya ramaṇāya namaḥ

Om! Prostrations to Ramana, who has eyes like blossoming lotuses

५५६ ॐ बन्धविमोचनाय रमणाय नमः

556 oṃ bandha-vimocanāya ramaṇāya namaḥ

Om! Prostrations to Ramana, who gives release from bondage

५५७ ॐ बहुप्रसादाय रमणाय नमः

557 oṃ bahu-prasādāya ramaṇāya namaḥ

Om! Prostrations to Ramana, who is highly gracious

५५८ ॐ बहुप्रदाय रमणाय नमः

558 oṃ bahu-pradāya ramaṇāya namaḥ

Om! Prostrations to Ramana, who gives in abundance

५५९ ॐ बहुज्ञातात्मज्ञानिने रमणाय नमः

559 oṃ bahu-jñāt-ātma-jñānine ramaṇāya namaḥ

Om! Prostrations to Ramana, who knows much [by] knowing the Self

५६० ॐ बान्धवाय रमणाय नमः

560 oṃ bāndhavāya ramaṇāya namaḥ

Om! Prostrations to Ramana, who is a friend

५६१ ॐ बाधोदासीनाय रमणाय नमः

561 oṃ bādho-dāsīnāya ramaṇāya namaḥ

Om! Prostrations to Ramana, who is indifferent to pain

५६२ ॐ बुधार्चिताय रमणाय नमः

562 oṃ budhārcitāya ramaṇāya namaḥ

Om! Prostrations to Ramana, who is worshipped by the knowledgeable, wise

५६३ ॐ बुधजनवन्दिताय रमणाय नमः

563 oṃ budha-jana-vanditāya ramaṇāya namaḥ

Om! Prostrations to Ramana to whom wise persons bow

५६४ ॐ बृहते रमणाय नमः

564 oṃ bṛhate ramaṇāya namaḥ

Om! Prostrations to Ramana, who is great

५६५ ॐ बृहत्पुराणपारायणाय रमणाय नमः

565 oṃ bṛhat-purāṇa-pārāyaṇāya ramaṇāya namaḥ

Om! Prostrations to Ramana, who read avidly the Periyapuranam

५६६ ॐ ब्रह्मचारिणे रमणाय नमः

566 oṃ brahmacāriṇe ramaṇāya namaḥ

Om! Prostrations to Ramana, the brahmacari, celibate student of Veda, one who moved in Brahman

५६७ ॐ ब्राह्मणस्वामिब्रह्मणे रमणाय नमः

567 oṃ brāhmaṇa-svāmi-brahmaṇe ramaṇāya namaḥ

Om! Prostrations to Ramana, the brahmin svami who is Brahman

५६८ ॐ ब्रह्मण्याय रमणाय नमः

568 oṃ brahmaṇyāya ramaṇāya namaḥ

Om! Prostrations to Ramana devoted to the Knowledge of Brahman

५६९ ॐ ब्रह्मविदे रमणाय नमः

569 oṃ brahma-vide ramaṇāya namaḥ

Om! Prostrations to Ramana, who knows Brahman

५७० ॐ ब्रह्मवर्चसे रमणाय नमः

570 oṃ brahma-varcase ramaṇāya namaḥ

Om! Prostrations to Ramana, who has Brahman splendour

५७१ ॐ ब्रह्मानन्दाय रमणाय नमः

571 oṃ brahmānandāya ramaṇāya namaḥ

Om! Prostrations to Ramana, who is in the bliss of Brahman

५७२ ॐ ब्रह्मौदनप्रियाय रमणाय नमः

572 oṃ brahmaudana-priyāya ramaṇāya namaḥ

Om! Prostrations to Ramana, who likes the Brahman food

५७३ ॐ ब्रह्मस्वरूपाय रमणाय नमः

573 oṃ brahma-svarūpāya ramaṇāya namaḥ

Om! Prostrations to Ramana, who is of the nature of Brahman

५७४ ॐ ब्रह्मणे रमणाय नमः

574 oṃ brahmaṇe ramaṇāya namaḥ

Om! Prostrations to Ramana, who is Brahman

५७५ ॐ भक्तप्रियाय रमणाय नमः

575 oṃ bhakta-priyāya ramaṇāya namaḥ

Om! Prostrations to Ramana, who is dear to the devotees

५७६ ॐ भक्तवत्सलाय रमणाय नमः

576 oṃ bhakta-vatsalāya ramaṇāya namaḥ

Om! Prostrations to Ramana, who has maternal love for the devotees

५७७ ॐ भक्तगणैरावृताय रमणाय नमः

577 oṃ bhakta-gaṇair-āvṛtāya ramaṇāya namaḥ

Om! Prostrations to Ramana, who is surrounded by the group of devotees

५७८ ॐ भक्तमन्दाराय रमणाय नमः

578 oṃ bhakta-mandārāya ramaṇāya namaḥ

Om! Prostrations to Ramana, who is a tree of paradise for his devotees

५७९ ॐ भक्तपराधीनाय रमणाय नमः

579 oṃ bhakta-parādhīnāya ramaṇāya namaḥ

Om! Prostrations to Ramana, who is bounden to the devotees

५८० ॐ भक्षणविशेषाणि सर्वं भक्तजनविनियोजि-
ताय रमणाय नमः

580 oṃ bhakṣaṇa-viśeṣāṇi sarvaṃ bhakta-jana-viniyojitāya ramaṇāya namaḥ

Om! Prostrations to Ramana, who distributes all the special sweets to the devotees

५८१ ॐ भक्तभारभृते रमणाय नमः

581 oṃ bhakta-bhāra-bhṛte ramaṇāya namaḥ

Om! Prostrations to Ramana, who bears the burden of the devotees

५८२ ॐ भक्तानुग्रहमूर्तये रमणाय नमः

582 oṃ bhakt-ānugraha-mūrtaye ramaṇāya namaḥ

Om! Prostrations to Ramana, the form that blesses, gives of his grace to, the devotees

५८३ ॐ भक्तरक्षणपरायणाय रमणाय नमः

583 oṃ bhakta-rakṣaṇa-parāyaṇāya ramaṇāya namaḥ

Om! Prostrations to Ramana, whose goal is the guarding of the devotees

५८४ ॐ भक्तावनप्रियाय रमणाय नमः

584 oṃ bhaktāvana-priyāya ramaṇāya namaḥ

Om! Prostrations to Ramana, who likes to protect his devotees

५८५ ॐ भक्तावनसमर्थाय रमणाय नमः

585 oṃ bhaktāvana-samarthāya ramaṇāya namaḥ

Om! Prostrations to Ramana, who is skilled in protecting devotees

५८६ ॐ भक्तजनहृदयविहाराय रमणाय नमः

586 oṃ bhakta-jana-hṛdaya-vihārāya ramaṇāya namaḥ

Om! Prostrations to Ramana, who roams about in the heart of his devotees

५८७ ॐ भक्तजनहृदयालयाय रमणाय नमः

587 oṃ bhakta-jana-hṛdayālayāya ramaṇāya namaḥ

Om! Prostrations to Ramana, who has as his abode the heart of his devotees

५८८ ॐ भक्तमानसहंसाय रमणाय नमः

588 oṃ bhakta-mānasa-haṃsāya ramaṇāya namaḥ

Om! Prostrations to Ramana, the swan that is in the Manasa lake, the minds, of the devotees

५८९ ॐ भक्तिज्ञानप्रदाय रमणाय नमः

589 oṃ bhakti-jñāna-pradāya ramaṇāya namaḥ

Om! Prostrations to Ramana, who confers devotion and knowledge

५९० ॐ भगवते रमणाय नमः

590 oṃ bhagavate ramaṇāya namaḥ

Om! Prostrations to Ramana, who is possessed of bhaga, which are the six qualities of power in full, prowess, glory, majesty, sacred knowledge, and indifference to the world

५९१ ॐ भवरोगभिषग्वराय रमणाय नमः

591 oṃ bhava-roga-bhiṣagvarāya ramaṇāya namaḥ

Om! Prostrations to Ramana, the best of doctors for the illness of worldly existence

५९२ ॐ भवरोगनिवारिणे रमणाय नमः

592 oṃ bhava-roga-nivāriṇe ramaṇāya namaḥ

Om! Prostrations to Ramana, who wards off the illness of worldly existence

५९३ ॐ भवबाधहराय रमणाय नमः

593 oṃ bhava-bādha-harāya ramaṇāya namaḥ

Om! Prostrations to Ramana, who takes away the pain of worldly existence

५९४ ॐ भवभयहराय रमणाय नमः

594 oṃ bhava-bhaya-harāya ramaṇāya namaḥ

Om! Prostrations to Ramana, who takes away the fear of worldly existence

५९५ ॐ भवभयभञ्जनाय रमणाय नमः

595 oṃ bhava-bhaya-bhañjanāya ramaṇāya namaḥ

Om! Prostrations to Ramana, who breaks up the fear of worldly existence

५९६ ॐ भवारण्यकुठारिकाय रमणाय नमः

596 oṃ bhavāraṇya-kuṭhārikāya ramaṇāya namaḥ

Om! Prostrations to Ramana, the axe for the forest of worldly existence

५९७ ॐ भवनाशनाय रमणाय नमः

597 oṃ bhava-nāśanāya ramaṇāya namaḥ

Om! Prostrations to Ramana, who destroys worldly existence

५९८ ॐ भवदावसुधावृष्टये रमणाय नमः

598 oṃ bhava-dāva-sudhā-vṛṣṭaye ramaṇāya namaḥ

Om! Prostrations to Ramana, the downpour of nectar for the forest fire of worldly existence

५९९ ॐ भवचक्रभञ्जनाय रमणाय नमः

599 oṃ bhava-cakra-bhañjanāya ramaṇāya namaḥ

Om! Prostrations to Ramana, who breaks the cycle of worldly existence

६०० ॐ भाग्यवर्धनाय रमणाय नमः

600 oṃ bhāgya-vardhanāya ramaṇāya namaḥ

Om! Prostrations to Ramana, who fosters happiness

६०१ ॐ भावनाय रमणाय नमः

601 oṃ bhāvanāya ramaṇāya namaḥ

Om! Prostrations to Ramana, who has conviction, displays, manifests

६०२ ॐ भावनागम्याय रमणाय नमः

602 oṃ bhāvanā-gamyāya ramaṇāya namaḥ

Om! Prostrations to Ramana, who is to be reached by conviction

६०३ ॐ भावपरायणाय रमणाय नमः

603 oṃ bhāva-parāyaṇāya ramaṇāya namaḥ

Om! Prostrations to Ramana, who is the goal of conviction

६०४ ॐ भावाभावविवर्जिताय रमणाय नमः

604 oṃ bhāv-ābhāva-vivarjitāya ramaṇāya namaḥ

Om! Prostrations to Ramana, who is devoid of existence and non-existence

६०५ ॐ भुक्तिमुक्तिस्वर्गापवर्गप्रदायकाय रमणाय नमः

605 oṃ bhukti-mukti-svargāpavarga-pradāyakāya ramaṇāya namaḥ

Om! Prostrations to Ramana, who confers experience, liberation, heaven and beyond

६०६ ॐ भूतावासाय रमणाय नमः

606 oṃ bhūt-āvāsāya ramaṇāya namaḥ

Om! Prostrations to Ramana, who dwells in the beings

६०७ ॐ भूतभविष्यद्भावविवर्जिताय रमणाय नमः

607 oṃ bhūta-bhaviṣyad-bhāva-vivarjitāya ramaṇāya namaḥ

Om! Prostrations to Ramana, who is devoid of the attitudes of the past and the future

६०८ ॐ भूमविद्याविशारदाय रमणाय नमः

608 oṃ bhūma-vidyā-viśāradāya ramaṇāya namaḥ

Om! Prostrations to Ramana, who is an expert in the knowledge of the abundant

६०९ ॐ भूमिनाथपुण्यक्षेत्रोत्थिताय रमणाय नमः

609 oṃ bhūminātha-puṇya-kṣetrotthitāya ramaṇāya namaḥ

Om! Prostrations to Ramana born in the holy center of Lord Bhuminatha (Lord of the Earth)

६१० ॐ भेदनाशिने रमणाय नमः

610 oṃ bheda-nāśine ramaṇāya namaḥ

Om! Prostrations to Ramana, who destroys differences

६११ ॐ भोगिने रमणाय नमः

611 oṃ bhogine ramaṇāya namaḥ

Om! Prostrations to Ramana, who enjoys

६१२ ॐ भ्रान्तिनाशनाय रमणाय नमः

612 oṃ bhrānti-nāśanāya ramaṇāya namaḥ

Om! Prostrations to Ramana, who destroys erroneous apprehensions

६१३ ॐ मकाराय रमणाय नमः

613 oṃ makārāya ramaṇāya namaḥ

Om! Prostrations to Ramana, who is of the nature of 'ma', the third letter of Om

६१४ ॐ मतिमते रमणाय नमः

614 oṃ mati-mate ramaṇāya namaḥ

Om! Prostrations to Ramana, who is intelligent

६१५ ॐ मतिदाय रमणाय नमः

615 oṃ mati-dāya ramaṇāya namaḥ

Om! Prostrations to Ramana, who confers intelligence

६१६ ॐ मत्यतीतमतये रमणाय नमः

616 oṃ maty-atīta-mataye ramaṇāya namaḥ

Om! Prostrations to Ramana, who has conviction transcending the intellect

६१७ ॐ मङ्गलदायकाय रमणाय नमः

617 oṃ maṅgala-dāyakāya ramaṇāya namaḥ

Om! Prostrations to Ramana, who gives success

६१८ ॐ मदनाशनाय रमणाय नमः

618 oṃ mada-nāśanāya ramaṇāya namaḥ

Om! Prostrations to Ramana, who destroys arrogance, conceit

६१९ ॐ मधुराय रमणाय नमः

619 oṃ madhurāya ramaṇāya namaḥ

Om! Prostrations to Ramana with a kind and friendly manner

६२० ॐ मधुरवचसे रमणाय नमः

620 oṃ madhura-vacase ramaṇāya namaḥ

Om! Prostrations to Ramana of sweet words

६२१ ॐ मधुपाय रमणाय नमः

621 oṃ madhupāya ramaṇāya namaḥ

Om! Prostrations to Ramana, who is like a bee

६२२ ॐ मधुरानगरविसर्जिताय रमणाय नमः

622 oṃ madhurā-nagara-visarjitāya ramaṇāya namaḥ

Om! Prostrations to Ramana, who came away from the town of Madura

६२३ ॐ मनोज्ञाय रमणाय नमः

623 oṃ manojñāya ramaṇāya namaḥ

Om! Prostrations to Ramana, who is charming

६२४ ॐ मनोहराय रमणाय नमः

624 oṃ manoharāya ramaṇāya namaḥ

Om! Prostrations to Ramana, who is captivating to the mind

६२५ ॐ मनोनाशकाय रमणाय नमः

625 oṃ mano-nāśakāya ramaṇāya namaḥ

Om! Prostrations to Ramana, who destroys the mind

६२६ ॐ मनोवेगाय रमणाय नमः

626 oṃ mano-vegāya ramaṇāya namaḥ

Om! Prostrations to Ramana, who has the speed of mind

६२७ ॐ मनोन्मनाय रमणाय नमः

627 oṃ manonmanāya ramaṇāya namaḥ

Om! Prostrations to Ramana, whose mind is turned inward, silent, inactive

६२८ ॐ मनोवाचामगोचराय रमणाय नमः

628 oṃ mano-vācām-agocarāya ramaṇāya namaḥ

Om! Prostrations to Ramana, who is beyond the range of mind and speech

६२९ ॐ मनोजवाय रमणाय नमः

629 oṃ mano-javāya ramaṇāya namaḥ

Om! Prostrations to Ramana, who is as fast as the mind

६३० ॐ मनस्विने रमणाय नमः

630 oṃ manasvine ramaṇāya namaḥ

Om! Prostrations to Ramana, the high-minded, the magnanimous

६३१ ॐ मन्त्राजपामूलाय रमणाय नमः

631 oṃ mantr-ājapā-mūlāya ramaṇāya namaḥ

Om! Prostrations to Ramana, who is the unuttered source of all mantra-s

६३२ ॐ मन्त्रपराय रमणाय नमः

632 oṃ mantraparāya ramaṇāya namaḥ

Om! Prostrations to Ramana, who is beyond mantra-s

६३३ ॐ मन्त्रालयाय रमणाय नमः

633 oṃ mantrālayāya ramaṇāya namaḥ

Om! Prostrations to Ramana, who is the abode of the mantra-s

६३४ ॐ मन्दस्मितप्रभाय रमणाय नमः

634 oṃ manda-smita-prabhāya ramaṇāya namaḥ

Om! Prostrations to Ramana, who has the radiance of a slight smile

६३५ ॐ मन्दहासाय रमणाय नमः

635 oṃ manda-hāsāya ramaṇāya namaḥ

Om! Prostrations to Ramana of soft laughter

६३६ ॐ मम मन रमणाय रमणाय नमः

636 oṃ mama mana ramaṇāya ramaṇāya namaḥ

Om! Prostrations to Ramana, who delights my mind

६३७ ॐ मयस्कराय रमणाय नमः

637 oṃ mayaskarāya ramaṇāya namaḥ

Om! Prostrations to Ramana, who gives happiness

६३८ ॐ मनोभुवे रमणाय नमः

638 oṃ manobhuve ramaṇāya namaḥ

Om! Prostrations to Ramana, who is the mind-born

६३९ ॐ मयूरप्रियाय रमणाय नमः

639 oṃ mayūra-priyāya ramaṇāya namaḥ

Om! Prostrations to Ramana, who loves peacocks

६४० ॐ मयूरपोषकाय रमणाय नमः

640 oṃ mayūra-poṣakāya ramaṇāya namaḥ

Om! Prostrations to Ramana, who nurtures peacocks

६४१ ॐ मयूरवाहनाय रमणाय नमः

641 oṃ mayūra-vāhanāya ramaṇāya namaḥ

Om! Prostrations to Ramana, who has the peacock as his mount

६४२ ॐ ममताहन्त्रे रमणाय नमः

642 oṃ mamatā-hantre ramaṇāya namaḥ

Om! Prostrations to Ramana, who destroys 'my-ness', the egoistic sense of possession

६४३ ॐ मरणानुभवाप्तनवजीवनाय रमणाय नमः

643 oṃ maraṇ-ānubhav-āpta-nava-jīvanāya ramaṇāya namaḥ

Om! Prostrations to Ramana, who obtained a new life out of an experience of death

६४४ ॐ महर्षये रमणाय नमः

644 oṃ maharṣaye ramaṇāya namaḥ

Om! Prostrations to Ramana, the great seer

६४५ ॐ महदव्यक्तादि स्वरूपाय रमणाय नमः

645 oṃ mahad-avyaktādi svarūpāya ramaṇāya namaḥ

Om! Prostrations to Ramana, who is of the nature of mahat (the first stage of creation), the unmanifest state and others

६४६ ॐ महाङ्गाय रमणाय नमः

646 oṃ mahāṅgāya ramaṇāya namaḥ

Om! Prostrations to Ramana of great characteristics

६४७ ॐ महाकायाय रमणाय नमः

647 oṃ mahā-kāyāya ramaṇāya namaḥ

Om! Prostrations to Ramana with a great body, also one who is the great bodiless

६४८ ॐ महनीयगुणात्मने रमणाय नमः

648 oṃ mahanīya-guṇātmane ramaṇāya namaḥ

Om! Prostrations to Ramana, who has in himself great qualities

६४९ ॐ महागीताय नमः

649 oṃ mahā-gītāya namaḥ

Om! Prostrations to Ramana of great songs

६५० ॐ महातेजस्विने रमणाय नमः

650 oṃ mahā-tejasvine ramaṇāya namaḥ

Om! Prostrations to Ramana, the highly effulgent

६५१ ॐ महावाक्यनिरूपणाय रमणाय नमः

651 oṃ mahā-vākya-nirūpaṇāya ramaṇāya namaḥ

Om! Prostrations to Ramana, who gives the definition of the mahavakya-s

६५२ ॐ महाज्वालाय रमणाय नमः

652 oṃ mahā-jvālāya ramaṇāya namaḥ

Om! Prostrations to Ramana, the great tongue of flame

६५३ ॐ महानेत्राय रमणाय नमः

653 oṃ mahā-netrāya ramaṇāya namaḥ

Om! Prostrations to Ramana with great eyes

६५४ ॐ महामूर्ध्ने रमणाय नमः

654 oṃ mahā-mūrdhne ramaṇāya namaḥ

Om! Prostrations to Ramana, who is the great summit

६५५ ॐ महाबुद्धये रमणाय नमः
655 oṃ mahā-buddhaye ramaṇāya namaḥ
Om! Prostrations to Ramana of great wisdom

६५६ ॐ महासिद्धये रमणाय नमः
656 oṃ mahā-siddhaye ramaṇāya namaḥ
Om! Prostrations to Ramana of great achievement

६५७ ॐ महापात्राय रमणाय नमः
657 oṃ mahā-pātrāya ramaṇāya namaḥ
Om! Prostrations to Ramana, who is a highly fit person

६५८ ॐ महामात्राय रमणाय नमः
658 oṃ mahā-mātrāya ramaṇāya namaḥ
Om! Prostrations to Ramana, the greatest, the best

६५९ ॐ महानिधये रमणाय नमः
659 oṃ mahā-nidhaye ramaṇāya namaḥ
Om! Prostrations to Ramana, the great treasure

६६० ॐ महायशसे रमणाय नमः
660 oṃ mahā-yaśase ramaṇāya namaḥ
Om! Prostrations to Ramana of great fame

६६१ ॐ महात्राणाय रमणाय नमः

661 oṃ mahā-trāṇāya ramaṇāya namaḥ

Om! Prostrations to Ramana, who is the great helper across

६६२ ॐ महाहर्षाय रमणाय नमः

662 oṃ mahā-harṣāya ramaṇāya namaḥ

Om! Prostrations to Ramana, who is in great happiness

६६३ ॐ महाहृदयाय रमणाय नमः

663 oṃ mahā-hṛdayāya ramaṇāya namaḥ

Om! Prostrations to Ramana with a great heart

६६४ ॐ महोदयाय रमणाय नमः

664 oṃ mahodayāya ramaṇāya namaḥ

Om! Prostrations to Ramana, the Lord, the master

६६५ ॐ महोत्साहाय रमणाय नमः

665 oṃ mahotsāhāya ramaṇāya namaḥ

Om! Prostrations to Ramana, the greatly enthusiastic [one]

६६६ ॐ महाशक्तये रमणाय नमः

666 oṃ mahā-śaktaye ramaṇāya namaḥ

Om! Prostrations to Ramana, the great power

६६७ ॐ महिमात्मने रमणाय नमः

667 oṃ mahimātmane ramaṇāya namaḥ

Om! Prostrations to Ramana, who has greatness in him

६६८ ॐ महीयसे रमणाय नमः

668 oṃ mahīyase ramaṇāya namaḥ

Om! Prostrations to Ramana, the very great

६६९ ॐ महौजसे रमणाय नमः

669 oṃ mahaujase ramaṇāya namaḥ

Om! Prostrations to Ramana, the great effulgence

६७० ॐ महामायासर्वनाशनाय रमणाय नमः

670 oṃ mahā-māyā-sarva-nāśanāya ramaṇāya namaḥ

Om! Prostrations to Ramana, the great destroyer of all illusion

६७१ ॐ महौषधाय रमणाय नमः

671 oṃ mahauṣadhāya ramaṇāya namaḥ

Om! Prostrations to Ramana, the great medicine

६७२ ॐ महायोगिने रमणाय नमः

672 oṃ mahā-yogine ramaṇāya namaḥ

Om! Prostrations to Ramana, the great yogi

६७३ ॐ महायोगेश्वराय रमणाय नमः

673 oṃ mahā-yogeśvarāya ramaṇāya namaḥ

Om! Prostrations to Ramana, the great lord of yoga

६७४ ॐ महासेनमहोंऽशेनजाताय रमणाय नमः

674 oṃ mahāsena-mahoṃ'śena-jātāya ramaṇāya namaḥ

Om! Prostrations to Ramana born with the effulgence of Mahasena (Skanda with a great army)

६७५ ॐ महान्तःप्रबोधेन आत्मज्ञानसंप्राप्ताय रमणाय नमः

675 oṃ mahāntaḥ-prabodhena ātma-jñāna-saṃprāptāya ramaṇāya namaḥ

Om! Prostrations to Ramana, who attained the Knowledge of the Self by the great awakening from within

६७६ ॐ महादेवाय रमणाय नमः

676 oṃ mahādevāya ramaṇāya namaḥ

Om! Prostrations to Ramana, the great God

६७७ ॐ महेश्वराय रमणाय नमः

677 oṃ maheśvarāya ramaṇāya namaḥ

Om! Prostrations to Ramana, the great Lord (Isvara)

६७८ ॐ मातृभ्रान्तिकल्पना हासकृताय रमणाय नमः

678 oṃ mātṛ-bhrānti-kalpanā hāsa-kṛtāya ramaṇāya namaḥ

Om! Prostrations to Ramana, who made the erroneous apprehensions of his mother a matter for laughter

६७९ ॐ मातृपितृगुरुरूपाय रमणाय नमः

679 oṃ mātṛ-pitṛ-guru-rūpāya ramaṇāya namaḥ

Om! Prostrations to Ramana, who is of the nature of mother, father, and guru

६८० ॐ मातृमुक्तिविधायकाय रमणाय नमः

680 oṃ mātṛ-mukti-vidhāyakāya ramaṇāya namaḥ

Om! Prostrations to Ramana, who brought about the liberation of his mother

६८१ ॐ मानवश्रेष्ठाय रमणाय नमः

681 oṃ mānava-śreṣṭāya ramaṇāya namaḥ

Om! Prostrations to Ramana, the best among men

६८२ ॐ मान्याय रमणाय नमः

682 oṃ mānyāya ramaṇāya namaḥ

Om! Prostrations to Ramana, who is to be revered

६८३ ॐ मात्सर्य-विनाशनाय रमणाय नमः

683 oṃ mātsarya-vināśanāya ramaṇāya namaḥ

Om! Prostrations to Ramana, who destroys jealousy

६८४ ॐ मायारहिताय रमणाय नमः

684 oṃ māyā-rahitāya ramaṇāya namaḥ

Om! Prostrations to Ramana, without delusion

६८५ ॐ मायाछेत्त्रे रमणाय नमः

685 oṃ māyā-chettre ramaṇāya namaḥ

Om! Prostrations to Ramana, who tears apart [the veil of] illusion

६८६ ॐ मायानाशनाय रमणाय नमः

686 oṃ māyā-nāśanāya ramaṇāya namaḥ

Om! Prostrations to Ramana, who destroys delusion

६८७ ॐ मायातीताय रमणाय नमः

687 oṃ māyātītāya ramaṇāya namaḥ

Om! Prostrations to Ramana, who transcends delusion

६८८ ॐ मायाविमोचनाय रमणाय नमः

688 oṃ māyā-vimocanāya ramaṇāya namaḥ

Om! Prostrations to Ramana, who delivers from delusion

६८९ ॐ मानसरहितहंसाय रमणाय नमः

689 oṃ mānasa-rahita-haṃsāya ramaṇāya namaḥ

Om! Prostrations to Ramana, the swan without its habitat the manasa lake, without its habitat the mind

६९० ॐ मार्गबन्धवे रमणाय नमः

690 oṃ mārga-bandhave ramaṇāya namaḥ

Om! Prostrations to Ramana, who is a friend on the way

६९१ ॐ मीढुष्टाय रमणाय नमः

691 oṃ mīḍhuṣṭāya ramaṇāya namaḥ

Om! Prostrations to Ramana, who gives bountifully

६९२ ॐ मुदितवदनाय रमणाय नमः

692 oṃ mudita-vadanāya ramaṇāya namaḥ

Om! Prostrations to Ramana with a happy face

६९३ ॐ मुनये रमणाय नमः

693 oṃ munaye ramaṇāya namaḥ

Om! Prostrations to Ramana, the sage

६९४ ॐ मुनीन्द्राय रमणाय नमः

694 oṃ munīndrāya ramaṇāya namaḥ

Om! Prostrations to Ramana, the lord of sages

६९५ ॐ मुण्डिने रमणाय नमः

695 oṃ muṇḍine ramaṇāya namaḥ

Om! Prostrations to Ramana with a shaven head

६९६ ॐ मुनिजनसेविताय रमणाय नमः

696 oṃ muni-jana-sevitāya ramaṇāya namaḥ

Om! Prostrations to Ramana, who is served by the congregation of sages

६९७ ॐ मुक्तिव्याख्यानिपुणाय रमणाय नमः

697 oṃ mukti-vyākhyā-nipuṇāya ramaṇāya namaḥ

Om! Prostrations to Ramana, who is adept at giving an exposition of liberation

६९८ ॐ मुक्तिप्रदाय रमणाय नमः

698 oṃ muktipradāya ramaṇāya namaḥ

Om! Prostrations to Ramana, who confers liberation

६९९ ॐ मुरुगनार्मुख्यबहुशिष्यस्तुताय रमणाय नमः

699 oṃ muruganār-mukhya-bahu-śiṣya-stutāya ramaṇāya namaḥ

Om! Prostrations to Ramana, who is praised by many devotees led by Muruganar

७०० ॐ मूलाधाराय रमणाय नमः

700 oṃ mūlādhārāya ramaṇāya namaḥ

Om! Prostrations to Ramana, who is the root support

७०१ ॐ मृत्युदारुकुठारिकाय रमणाय नमः

701 oṃ mṛtyu-dāru-kuṭhārikāya ramaṇāya namaḥ

Om! Prostrations to Ramana, the axe for the tree of death

७०२ ॐ मृत्युञ्जयाय रमणाय नमः

702 oṃ mṛtyuñ-jayāya ramaṇāya namaḥ

Om! Prostrations to Ramana, who has conquered death

७०३ ॐ मृदुभाषिणे रमणाय नमः

703 oṃ mṛdu-bhāṣiṇe ramaṇāya namaḥ

Om! Prostrations to Ramana of sweet talk

७०४ ॐ मोहनाशनाय रमणाय नमः

704 oṃ moha-nāśanāya ramaṇāya namaḥ

Om! Prostrations to Ramana, who destroys stupefaction, delusion

७०५ ॐ मौनगुरवे रमणाय नमः

705 oṃ mauna-gurave ramaṇāya namaḥ

Om! Prostrations to Ramana, the silent Guru

७०६ ॐ मौनलीलाय रमणाय नमः

706 oṃ mauna-līlāya ramaṇāya namaḥ

Om! Prostrations to Ramana, whose play is silence

७०७ ॐ मौनमूर्तये रमणाय नमः

707 oṃ mauna-mūrtaye ramaṇāya namaḥ

Om! Prostrations to Ramana, the form of silence

७०८ ॐ मौनस्वात्मबोधकाय रमणाय नमः

708 oṃ mauna-svātma-bodhakāya ramaṇāya namaḥ

Om! Prostrations to Ramana, the silent instructor of one's own Self

७०९ ॐ मौनव्याख्याप्रकटितपरात्मतत्त्वाय रमणाय नमः

709 oṃ mauna-vyākhyā-prakaṭita-parātma-tattvāya ramaṇāya namaḥ

Om! Prostrations to Ramana, who gives a silent exposition of the supreme Truth of the Self

७१० ॐ मौनस्वभावाय रमणाय नमः

710 oṃ mauna-svabhāvāya ramaṇāya namaḥ

Om! Prostrations to Ramana, whose nature is silence

७११ ॐ यमाय रमणाय नमः

711 oṃ yamāya ramaṇāya namaḥ

Om! Prostrations to Ramana, who is disciplined, also the Lord of death

७१२ ॐ यमशिक्षानिवारणाय रमणाय नमः

712 oṃ yama-śikṣā-nivāraṇāya ramaṇāya namaḥ

Om! Prostrations to Ramana, who prevents the punishment by the Lord of death

७१३ ॐ यशस्विने रमणाय नमः

713 oṃ yaśasvine ramaṇāya namaḥ

Om! Prostrations to Ramana, who is famous

७१४ ॐ युगपुरुषाय रमणाय नमः

714 oṃ yuga-puruṣāya ramaṇāya namaḥ

Om! Prostrations to Ramana, the man of the yuga

७१५ ॐ योग्याय रमणाय नमः

715 oṃ yogyāya ramaṇāya namaḥ

Om! Prostrations to Ramana, the one who is trustworthy, one who could be united with

७१६ ॐ योगनिधये रमणाय नमः

716 oṃ yoga-nidhaye ramaṇāya namaḥ

Om! Prostrations to Ramana, the treasure of yoga

७१७ ॐ योगीश्वरवन्दिताय रमणाय नमः

717 oṃ yogīśvara-vanditāya ramaṇāya namaḥ

Om! Prostrations to Ramana, who is worshipped by the yogi-masters

७१८ ॐ योगाध्यक्षाय रमणाय नमः

718 oṃ yogādhyakṣāya ramaṇāya namaḥ

Om! Prostrations to Ramana, the teacher of yoga

७१९ ॐ योगक्षेमवहाय रमणाय नमः

719 oṃ yoga-kṣema-vahāya ramaṇāya namaḥ

Om! Prostrations to Ramana, who bears, takes charge of, welfare

७२० ॐ रचिताचलताण्डवाय रमणाय नमः

720 oṃ racitācala-tāṇḍavāya ramaṇāya namaḥ

Om! Prostrations to Ramana, who relishes the dance of the mountain, dance on the mountain

७२१ ॐ रमणाय रमणाय नमः

721 oṃ ramaṇāya ramaṇāya namaḥ

Om! Prostrations to Ramana, one who delights

७२२ ॐ रमणीयाय रमणाय नमः

722 oṃ ramaṇīyāya ramaṇāya namaḥ

Om! Prostrations to Ramana, who gives enjoyment

७२३ ॐ रमणीयवचसे रमणाय नमः

723 oṃ ramaṇīya-vacase ramaṇāya namaḥ

Om! Prostrations to Ramana of engaging conversation, enjoyable talk

७२४ ॐ रमणाश्रमदेवाय रमणाय नमः

724 oṃ ramaṇāśrama-devāya ramaṇāya namaḥ

Om! Prostrations to Ramana, the god of Ramanasramam

७२५ ॐ रमणकेन्द्रपूजिताय रमणाय नमः

725 oṃ ramaṇakendrapūjitāya ramaṇāya namaḥ

Om! Prostrations to Ramana, who is worshipped in Ramana kendra-s

७२६ ॐ रसज्ञाय रमणाय नमः

726 oṃ rasajñāya ramaṇāya namaḥ

Om! Prostrations to Ramana, who knows the essence

७२७ ॐ रागद्वेषविनाशकाय रमणाय नमः

727 oṃ rāga-dveṣa-vināśakāya ramaṇāya namaḥ

Om! Prostrations to Ramana, who destroys passion and hatred

७२८ ॐ रागमथनाय रमणाय नमः

728 oṃ rāga-mathanāya ramaṇāya namaḥ

Om! Prostrations to Ramana, who stamps out passion

७२९ ॐ राजाधिराजाय रमणाय नमः

729 oṃ rājādhi-rājāya ramaṇāya namaḥ

Om! Prostrations to Ramana, the king over kings

७३० ॐ लयकराय रमणाय नमः

730 oṃ laya-karāya ramaṇāya namaḥ

Om! Prostrations to Ramana, who brings about dissolution

७३१ ॐ लोभनाशनाय रमणाय नमः

731 oṃ lobha-nāśanāya ramaṇāya namaḥ

Om! Prostrations to Ramana, who destroys greed

७३२ ॐ लोकहिताय रमणाय नमः

732 oṃ loka-hitāya ramaṇāya namaḥ

Om! Prostrations to Ramana, who is beneficial to the world

७३३ ॐ लोकबान्धवाय रमणाय नमः

733 oṃ loka-bāndhavāya ramaṇāya namaḥ

Om! Prostrations to Ramana, the friend of the world

७३४ ॐ लोकवन्दिताय रमणाय नमः

734 oṃ loka-vanditāya ramaṇāya namaḥ

Om! Prostrations to Ramana to whom the world bows

७३५ ॐ लोकनाथाय रमणाय नमः

735 oṃ loka-nāthāya ramaṇāya namaḥ

Om! Prostrations to Ramana, the Lord of the world

७३६ ॐ वन्द्याय रमणाय नमः

736 oṃ vandyāya ramaṇāya namaḥ

Om! Prostrations to Ramana, who is to be bowed to

७३७ ॐ वन्दारुजनवत्सलाय रमणाय नमः

737 oṃ vandāru-jana-vatsalāya ramaṇāya namaḥ

Om! Prostrations to Ramana, who has motherly benevolence towards the people who worship

७३८ ॐ वराय रमणाय नमः

738 oṃ varāya ramaṇāya namaḥ

Om! Prostrations to Ramana, the superior

७३९ ॐ वरगुणाय रमणाय नमः

739 oṃ vara-guṇāya ramaṇāya namaḥ

Om! Prostrations to Ramana of superior qualities

७४० ॐ वरज्ञानाय रमणाय नमः

740 oṃ varajñānāya ramaṇāya namaḥ

Om! Prostrations to Ramana of superior knowledge

७४१ ॐ वरेण्याय रमणाय नमः

741 oṃ vareṇyāya ramaṇāya namaḥ

Om! Prostrations to Ramana, who is to be wished for, desired

७४२ ॐ वरिष्ठाय रमणाय नमः

742 oṃ variṣṭāya ramaṇāya namaḥ

Om! Prostrations to Ramana, the best

७४३ ॐ वरशान्ताय रमणाय नमः

743 oṃ vara-śāntāya ramaṇāya namaḥ

Om! Prostrations to Ramana, who is of superior, exceptional, patience

७४४ ॐ वशाकराय रमणाय नमः

744 oṃ vaśa-karāya ramaṇāya namaḥ

Om! Prostrations to Ramana, who creates attraction

७४५ ॐ वशिने रमणाय नमः

745 oṃ vaśine ramaṇāya namaḥ

Om! Prostrations to Ramana, who captivates

७४६ ॐ वटुवेषोपवीतविसर्जिताय रमणाय नमः

746 oṃ vaṭu-veṣopavīta-visarjitāya ramaṇāya namaḥ

Om! Prostrations to Ramana, who cast off the sacred thread indicating the mark of a brahmin boy

७४७ ॐ वर्चस्विने रमणाय नमः

747 oṃ varcasvine ramaṇāya namaḥ

Om! Prostrations to Ramana of great energy

७४८ ॐ वाचस्पतये रमणाय नमः

748 oṃ vācaspataye ramaṇāya namaḥ

Om! Prostrations to Ramana, the master of speech

७४९ ॐ वागीश्वराय रमणाय नमः

749 oṃ vāgīśvarāya ramaṇāya namaḥ

Om! Prostrations to Ramana, the lord of speech

७५० ॐ विनताय रमणाय नमः

750 oṃ vinatāya ramaṇāya namaḥ

Om! Prostrations to Ramana, who is humble

५१ ॐ विनुताय रमणाय नमः

751 oṃ vinutāya ramaṇāya namaḥ

Om! Prostrations to Ramana, who is saluted

७५२ ॐ विमलाय रमणाय नमः

752 oṃ vimalāya ramaṇāya namaḥ

Om! Prostrations to Ramana, the blemishless

७५३ ॐ विजयाक्षाय रमणाय नमः

753 oṃ vijayākṣāya ramaṇāya namaḥ

Om! Prostrations to Ramana with eyes that conquer

७५४ ॐ विदग्धाय रमणाय नमः

754 oṃ vidagdhāya ramaṇāya namaḥ

Om! Prostrations to Ramana, who is clever, a scholar, skilled, artful

७५५ ॐ विद्यादायिने रमणाय नमः

755 oṃ vidyā-dāyine ramaṇāya namaḥ

Om! Prostrations to Ramana, who confers learning, knowledge

७५६ ॐ विबुधाय रमणाय नमः

756 oṃ vibudhāya ramaṇāya namaḥ

Om! Prostrations to Ramana, the highly learned, knowledgeable

७५७ ॐ विबुधप्रियाय रमणाय नमः

757 oṃ vibudha-priyāya ramaṇāya namaḥ

Om! Prostrations to Ramana, who is dear to the highly learned, those who know

७५८ ॐ विबुधाश्रयाय रमणाय नमः

758 oṃ vibudh-āśrayāya ramaṇāya namaḥ

Om! Prostrations to Ramana, who is the support of the highly learned

७५९ ॐ विभवे रमणाय नमः

759 oṃ vibhave ramaṇāya namaḥ

Om! Prostrations to Ramana, the glorious one

७६० ॐ विप्राय रमणाय नमः

760 oṃ viprāya ramaṇāya namaḥ

Om! Prostrations to Ramana, the sage

७६१ ॐ विप्रप्रियाय रमणाय नमः

761 oṃ vipra-priyāya ramaṇāya namaḥ

Om! Prostrations to Ramana dear to the learned brahmins

७६२ ॐ विप्रप्रसादाय रमणाय नमः

762 oṃ vipra-prasādāya ramaṇāya namaḥ

Om! Prostrations to Ramana, who is gracious to the learned brahmins

७६३ ॐ विज्ञात्रे रमणाय नमः

763 oṃ vijñātre ramaṇāya namaḥ

Om! Prostrations to Ramana, who knows

७६४ ॐ विज्ञानकलनाय रमणाय नमः

764 oṃ vijñāna-kalanāya ramaṇāya namaḥ

Om! Prostrations to Ramana, who activates knowledge

७६५ ॐ विकल्पपरिवर्जिताय रमणाय नमः

765 oṃ vikalpa-parivarjitāya ramaṇāya namaḥ

Om! Prostrations to Ramana, who is devoid of erroneous thoughts

७६६ ॐ विद्वेषणहराय रमणाय नमः

766 oṃ vidveṣaṇa-harāya ramaṇāya namaḥ

Om! Prostrations to Ramana, who destroys enmity

७६७ ॐ विमोचनाय रमणाय नमः

767 oṃ vimocanāya ramaṇāya namaḥ

Om! Prostrations to Ramana, who gives deliverance

७६८ ॐ वियत्कल्पाय रमणाय नमः

768 oṃ viyat-kalpāya ramaṇāya namaḥ

Om! Prostrations to Ramana, who is akin to space

७६९ ॐ विदेशविशेषपूजिताय रमणाय नमः

769 oṃ videśa-viśeṣa-pūjitāya ramaṇāya namaḥ

Om! Prostrations to Ramana, who is well worshipped in foreign countries

७७० ॐ विभाषानुवाद् विचक्षणाय रमणाय नमः

770 oṃ vibhāṣānuvāda vicakṣaṇāya ramaṇāya namaḥ

Om! Prostrations to Ramana, who is the master of translation into other languages

७७१ ॐ विद्रुमशैलस्थाय रमणाय नमः

771 oṃ vidruma-śaila-sthāya ramaṇāya namaḥ

Om! Prostrations to Ramana, who stayed on the Coral Hill (Pavalakkunru)

७७२ ॐ विरजाय रमणाय नमः

772 oṃ virajāya ramaṇāya namaḥ

Om! Prostrations to Ramana, who is free of dust

७७३ ॐ विराजिताय रमणाय नमः

773 oṃ virājitāya ramaṇāya namaḥ

Om! Prostrations to Ramana, who is brilliant

७७४ ॐ विराजदचलाकृतये रमणाय नमः

774 oṃ virājad-acalākṛtaye ramaṇāya namaḥ

Om! Prostrations to Ramana shining in the form of a mountain

७७५ ॐ विरागिणे रमणाय नमः

775 oṃ virāgiṇe ramaṇāya namaḥ

Om! Prostrations to Ramana, without passion, without attachment

७७६ ॐ विरामाय रमणाय नमः

776 oṃ virāmāya ramaṇāya namaḥ

Om! Prostrations to Ramana, who is in repose

७७७ ॐ विवेकबोधकाय रमणाय नमः

777 oṃ viveka-bodhakāya ramaṇāya namaḥ

Om! Prostrations to Ramana, who teaches discrimination

७७८ ॐ विरूपाक्षगुहावासाय रमणाय नमः

778 oṃ virūpākṣa-guhā-vāsāya ramaṇāya namaḥ

Om! Prostrations to Ramana, who lived in the Virupaksa cave

७७९ ॐ विशिष्टाय रमणाय नमः

779 oṃ viśiṣṭāya ramaṇāya namaḥ

Om! Prostrations to Ramana, the distinguished

७८० ॐ विशालदृष्टये रमणाय नमः

780 oṃ viśāla-dṛṣṭaye ramaṇāya namaḥ

Om! Prostrations to Ramana of far-seeing vision

७८१ ॐ विशालहृदयाय रमणाय नमः

781 oṃ viśāla-hṛdayāya ramaṇāya namaḥ

Om! Prostrations to Ramana, the large-hearted

७८२ ॐ विशुद्धात्मने रमणाय नमः

782 oṃ viśuddhātmane ramaṇāya namaḥ

Om! Prostrations to Ramana, the pure Self

७८३ ॐ विश्वम्बराय रमणाय नमः

783 oṃ viśvambarāya ramaṇāya namaḥ

Om! Prostrations to Ramana, who is all sustaining, all-bearing

७८४ ॐ विश्ववन्द्याय रमणाय नमः

784 oṃ viśva-vandyāya ramaṇāya namaḥ

Om! Prostrations to Ramana, who is to be worshipped by the universe

७८५ ॐ विस्मयरूपाय रमणाय नमः

785 oṃ vismaya-rūpāya ramaṇāya namaḥ

Om! Prostrations to Ramana of wonderful form

७८६ ॐ विश्वमूर्तये रमणाय नमः

786 oṃ viśva-mūrtaye ramaṇāya namaḥ

Om! Prostrations to Ramana of the form of the universe

७८७ ॐ विश्वेश्वराय रमणाय नमः

787 oṃ viśveśvarāya ramaṇāya namaḥ

Om! Prostrations to Ramana, the Lord of the universe

७८८ ॐ विदेशविश्रुतज्ञानिने रमणाय नमः

788 oṃ videśa-viśruta-jñānine ramaṇāya namaḥ

Om! Prostrations to Ramana, the sage who is well known in other countries

७८९ ॐ वेङ्कटरामाय रमणाय नमः

789 oṃ veṅkaṭarāmāya ramaṇāya namaḥ

Om! Prostrations to Ramana, [named Sri] Venkatarama

७९० ॐ वेदघोषप्रियाय रमणाय नमः

790 oṃ veda-ghoṣa-priyāya ramaṇāya namaḥ

Om! Prostrations to Ramana, who likes vedic chanting

७९१ ॐ वेदवेदान्तवेद्याय रमणाय नमः

791 oṃ veda-vedānta-vedyāya ramaṇāya namaḥ

Om! Prostrations to Ramana, who is to be known through the veda-s and vedanta

७९२ ॐ वेदवेदान्ततत्त्वार्थाय रमणाय नमः

792 oṃ veda-vedānta-tattvārthāya ramaṇāya namaḥ

Om! Prostrations to Ramana, who is the true meaning of the veda-s and vedanta

७९३ ॐ वेदान्तसाराय रमणाय नमः

793 oṃ vedānta-sārāya ramaṇāya namaḥ

Om! Prostrations to Ramana, who is the essence of the vedanta

७९४ ॐ वेदपुरुषाय रमणाय नमः

794 oṃ veda-puruṣāya ramaṇāya namaḥ

Om! Prostrations to Ramana, the embodiment of the veda-s

७९५ ॐ वेद्यवर्जिताय रमणाय नमः

795 oṃ vedya-varjitāya ramaṇāya namaḥ

Om! Prostrations to Ramana, who has nothing to learn

७९६ ॐ वैदम्भाय रमणाय नमः

796 oṃ vaidambhāya ramaṇāya namaḥ

Om! Prostrations to Ramana without hypocrisy

७९७ ॐ व्यक्ताव्यक्ताय रमणाय नमः

797 oṃ vyaktāvyaktāya ramaṇāya namaḥ

Om! Prostrations to Ramana, who is the manifest and unmanifest

७९८ ॐ व्यापकाय रमणाय नमः

798 oṃ vyāpakāya ramaṇāya namaḥ

Om! Prostrations to Ramana, who is pervasive

७९९ ॐ व्योमवत्व्याप्ताय रमणाय नमः

799 oṃ vyomavat-vyāptāya ramaṇāya namaḥ

Om! Prostrations to Ramana, who is pervasive like the sky

८०० ॐ शंकराय रमणाय नमः

800 oṃ śaṃkarāya ramaṇāya namaḥ

Om! Prostrations to Ramana, who does auspicious things, Sankara

८०१ ॐ शक्तिधराय रमणाय नमः

801 oṃ śakti-dharāya ramaṇāya namaḥ

Om! Prostrations to Ramana, who wields the Sakti, the divine power

८०२ ॐ शमान्विताय रमणाय नमः

802 oṃ śamānvitāya ramaṇāya namaḥ

Om! Prostrations to Ramana, who is endowed with tranquility

८०३ ॐ शरण्याय रमणाय नमः

803 oṃ śaraṇyāya ramaṇāya namaḥ

Om! Prostrations to Ramana to whom one should surrender

८०४ ॐ शान्तस्वरूपाय रमणाय नमः

804 oṃ śānta-svarūpāya ramaṇāya namaḥ

Om! Prostrations to Ramana, who is peace personified

८०५ ॐ शान्तमूर्तये रमणाय नमः

805 oṃ śānta-mūrtaye ramaṇāya namaḥ

Om! Prostrations to Ramana, the embodiment of peace

८०६ ॐ शान्तसंकल्पाय रमणाय नमः

806 oṃ śānta-saṃkalpāya ramaṇāya namaḥ

Om! Prostrations to Ramana, who has peace as his sankalpa

८०७ ॐ शान्तिदेवाय रमणाय नमः

807 oṃ śānti-devāya ramaṇāya namaḥ

Om! Prostrations to Ramana, the God of peace

८०८ ॐ शाश्वताय रमणाय नमः

808 oṃ śāśvatāya ramaṇāya namaḥ

Om! Prostrations to Ramana, the permanent

८०९ ॐ शिपिविष्टाय रमणाय नमः

809 oṃ śipi-viṣṭāya ramaṇāya namaḥ

Om! Prostrations to Ramana, the bald headed, one pervaded by rays

८१० ॐ शिवाय रमणाय नमः

810 oṃ śivāya ramaṇāya namaḥ

Om! Prostrations to Ramana, all peace, beatitude, Siva

८११ ॐ शिष्टपरिपालनाय रमणाय नमः

811 oṃ śiṣṭa-paripālanāya ramaṇāya namaḥ

Om! Prostrations to Ramana, who takes care of wise people

८१२ ॐ शुचये रमणाय नमः

812 oṃ śucaye ramaṇāya namaḥ

Om! Prostrations to Ramana, the immaculate one

८१३ ॐ शुद्धमानसाय रमणाय नमः

813 oṃ śuddha-mānasāya ramaṇāya namaḥ

Om! Prostrations to Ramana with a pure mind

८१४ ॐ शुद्धात्मने रमणाय नमः

814 oṃ śuddhātmane ramaṇāya namaḥ

Om! Prostrations to Ramana, the pure Self

८१५ ॐ शुद्धसत्त्वस्थिताय रमणाय नमः

815 oṃ śuddha-sattva-sthitāya ramaṇāya namaḥ

Om! Prostrations to Ramana, who is established in pure truth

८१६ ॐ शुभाय रमणाय नमः

816 oṃ śubhāya ramaṇāya namaḥ

Om! Prostrations to Ramana, the auspicious

८१७ ॐ शुभाक्षाय रमणाय नमः

817 oṃ śubhākṣāya ramaṇāya namaḥ

Om! Prostrations to Ramana with the auspicious eye

८१८ ॐ शुभ्रवस्त्राय रमणाय नमः

818 oṃ śubhra-vastrāya ramaṇāya namaḥ

Om! Prostrations to Ramana with white clothes

८१९ ॐ शुभ्रकौपीनधारिणे रमणाय नमः

819 oṃ śubhra-kaupīna-dhāriṇe ramaṇāya namaḥ

Om! Prostrations to Ramana wearing the bright white loin cloth

८२० ॐ शोकनाशनाय रमणाय नमः

820 oṃ śoka-nāśanāya ramaṇāya namaḥ

Om! Prostrations to Ramana, who destroys sadness

८२१ ॐ शोभनाय रमणाय नमः

821 oṃ śobhanāya ramaṇāya namaḥ

Om! Prostrations to Ramana, who confers auspiciousness

८२२ ॐ शोणाचलमहोलीनमानसाय रमणाय नमः

822 oṃ śoṇācala-maho-līna-mānasāya ramaṇāya namaḥ

Om! Prostrations to Ramana, whose mind was absorbed in the effulgence that is the mountain Arunachala

८२३ ॐ शोभनदुर्मुखि सिंहमासे शोणशैलमागताय रमणाय नमः

823 oṃ śobhana-durmukhi siṃha-māse śoṇa-śailam-āgatāya ramaṇāya namaḥ

Om! Prostrations to Ramana, who came to Arunachala in the month of Simha in the auspicious year of Durmukhi

८२४ ॐ श्वेताम्बराय रमणाय नमः

824 oṃ śvetāmbarāya ramaṇāya namaḥ

Om! Prostrations to Ramana, who has white clothes

८२५ ॐ श्रुतिसंपन्नाय रमणाय नमः

825 oṃ śruti-saṃpannāya ramaṇāya namaḥ

Om! Prostrations to Ramana, who is endowed with the veda-s

८२६ ॐ श्रुतिसागराय रमणाय नमः

826 oṃ śruti-sāgarāya ramaṇāya namaḥ

Om! Prostrations to Ramana, who is the ocean of veda-s

८२७ ॐ श्रेष्ठाय रमणाय नमः

827 oṃ śreṣṭāya ramaṇāya namaḥ

Om! Prostrations to Ramana, the best

८२८ ॐ श्रितजनपालकाय रमणाय नमः

828 oṃ śrita-jana-pālakāya ramaṇāya namaḥ

Om! Prostrations to Ramana, who gives protection to those who take refuge in him

८२९ ॐ सर्वतः संप्लुतोदकात्मनि उदपानकृत वेदशास्त्राय रमणाय नमः

829 oṃ sarvataḥ saṃplutodak-ātmani udapāna-kṛta veda-śāstrāya ramaṇāya namaḥ

Om! Prostrations to Ramana, who has made a limited well of veda sastra-s in the flood of Atma all around

८३० ॐ संकल्पहीनाय रमणाय नमः

830 oṃ saṃkalpa-hīnāya ramaṇāya namaḥ

Om! Prostrations to Ramana devoid of sankalpa

८३१ ॐ संकटहराय रमणाय नमः

831 oṃ saṃkaṭa-harāya ramaṇāya namaḥ

Om! Prostrations to Ramana, who removes difficulties

८३२ ॐ सकलाय रमणाय नमः

832 oṃ sakalāya ramaṇāya namaḥ

Om! Prostrations to Ramana, who is everything

८३३ ॐ सच्चिदानन्दस्वरूपाय रमणाय नमः

833 oṃ saccidānanda-svarūpāya ramaṇāya namaḥ

Om! Prostrations to Ramana, who is of the nature of Being, Consciousness, Bliss

८३४ ॐ संतृप्ताय रमणाय नमः

834 oṃ saṃtṛptāya ramaṇāya namaḥ

Om! Prostrations to Ramana, who is well satisfied

८३५ ॐ समपङ्क्तिभोजनप्रियाय रमणाय नमः

835 oṃ sama-paṅkti-bhojana-priyāya ramaṇāya namaḥ

Om! Prostrations to Ramana, who likes eating in company as an equal

८३६ ॐ संयताय रमणाय नमः

836 oṃ saṃyatāya ramaṇāya namaḥ

Om! Prostrations to Ramana, who is ready

८३७ ॐ संशयघ्ने रमणाय नमः

837 oṃ saṃśayaghne ramaṇāya namaḥ

Om! Prostrations to Ramana, who destroys doubt

८३८ ॐ संराजे रमणाय नमः

838 oṃ saṃrāje ramaṇāya namaḥ

Om! Prostrations to Ramana, the king of all

८३९ ॐ संसारार्णवतारकाय रमणाय नमः

839 oṃ saṃsār-ārṇava-tārakāya ramaṇāya namaḥ

Om! Prostrations to Ramana, who helps across the ocean of samsara

८४० ॐ संसाररहिताय रमणाय नमः

840 oṃ saṃsāra-rahitāya ramaṇāya namaḥ

Om! Prostrations to Ramana, who is without samsara

८४१ ॐ संसारचक्रभञ्जनचक्रवर्तिने रमणाय नमः

841 oṃ saṃsāra-cakra-bhañjana-cakravartine ramaṇāya namaḥ

Om! Prostrations to Ramana, the emperor who shatters the wheel of samsara

८४२ ॐ संतुष्टाय रमणाय नमः

842 oṃ saṃtuṣṭāya ramaṇāya namaḥ

Om! Prostrations to Ramana, who is happy

८४३ ॐ सत्याय रमणाय नमः

843 oṃ satyāya ramaṇāya namaḥ

Om! Prostrations to Ramana, who is truthful

८४४ ॐ सते रमणाय नमः

844 oṃ sate ramaṇāya namaḥ

Om! Prostrations to Ramana, who is the Truth

८४५ ॐ सत्यसंघाय रमणाय नमः

845 oṃ satya-saṃghāya ramaṇāya namaḥ

Om! Prostrations to Ramana, who is attached to the Truth

८४६ ॐ सत्यव्रताय रमणाय नमः

846 oṃ satya-vratāya ramaṇāya namaḥ

Om! Prostrations to Ramana, who has the vow of Truth

८४७ ॐ सत्यवच्चसे रमणाय नमः

847 oṃ satya-vacase ramaṇāya namaḥ

Om! Prostrations to Ramana of truthful words

८४८ ॐ सत्यसंकल्पाय रमणाय नमः

848 oṃ satya-saṃkalpāya ramaṇāya namaḥ

Om! Prostrations to Ramana of truthful resolve

८४९ ॐ सत्यज्ञानपरायणाय रमणाय नमः

849 oṃ satya-jñāna-parāyaṇāya ramaṇāya namaḥ

Om! Prostrations to Ramana, who is devoted to Truth and Knowledge, True Knowledge

८५० ॐ सदाचारविचारप्रवर्तकाय नमः

850 oṃ sad-ācāra-vicāra-pravartakāya namaḥ

Om! Prostrations to Ramana, who spreads inquiry into true tradition

८५१ ॐ सद्गतिप्रदायकाय रमणाय नमः

851 oṃ sad-gati-pradāyakāya ramaṇāya namaḥ

Om! Prostrations to Ramana, who shows the goal of Truth

८५२ ॐ सत्यतत्त्वबोधकाय रमणाय नमः

852 oṃ satya-tattva-bodhakāya ramaṇāya namaḥ

Om! Prostrations to Ramana, who teaches the principle of Truth

८५३ ॐ सत्यरूपाय रमणाय नमः

853 oṃ satya-rūpāya ramaṇāya namaḥ

Om! Prostrations to Ramana, who is of the nature of Truth

८५४ ॐ सत्यधामाय रमणाय नमः

854 oṃ satya-dhāmāya ramaṇāya namaḥ

Om! Prostrations to Ramana, who is in the abode of Truth

८५५ ॐ सत्यसंघपूजिताय रमणाय नमः

855 oṃ satya-saṃgha-pūjitāya ramaṇāya namaḥ

Om! Prostrations to Ramana, who is worshipped in the company of the truthful

८५६ ॐ सत्यसंघप्रियाय रमणाय नमः

856 oṃ satya-saṃgha-priyāya ramaṇāya namaḥ

Om! Prostrations to Ramana, who likes the company of the truthful

८५७ ॐ सद्यप्रसादिने रमणाय नमः

857 oṃ sadya-prasādine ramaṇāya namaḥ

Om! Prostrations to Ramana, who confers grace instantly, is pleased instantly

८५८ ॐ सदातुष्टाय रमणाय नमः

858 oṃ sadā-tuṣṭāya ramaṇāya namaḥ

Om! Prostrations to Ramana, who is ever happy

८५९ ॐ सदानन्दाय रमणाय नमः

859 oṃ sadānandāya ramaṇāya namaḥ

Om! Prostrations to Ramana, who is ever in bliss

८६० ॐ सदसते रमणाय नमः

860 oṃ sadasate ramaṇāya namaḥ

Om! Prostrations to Ramana, who is both the Real and the unreal

८६१ ॐ सदात्मविरामाय रमणाय नमः

861 oṃ sadātma-virāmāya ramaṇāya namaḥ

Om! Prostrations to Ramana, who is ever reposing in the Self

८६२ ॐ सदसस्पतये रमणाय नमः

862 oṃ sadasas-pataye ramaṇāya namaḥ

Om! Prostrations to Ramana, the leader of the assembly

८६३ ॐ संदेहनिवारिणे रमणाय नमः

863 oṃ saṃdeha-nivāriṇe ramaṇāya namaḥ

Om! Prostrations to Ramana, who clears up doubts, wards off doubts

८६४ ॐ सनकादिसमानाय रमणाय नमः

864 oṃ sanakādi-samānāya ramaṇāya namaḥ

Om! Prostrations to Ramana, who equals the sages Sanaka and others (mind-born sons of Brahma)

८६५ ॐ सनातनाय रमणाय नमः

865 oṃ sanātanāya ramaṇāya namaḥ

Om! Prostrations to Ramana, who is immemorial

८६६ ॐ सनातनधर्मचर्याय रमणाय नमः

866 oṃ sanātana-dharma-caryāya ramaṇāya namaḥ

Om! Prostrations to Ramana, who follows the immemorial tradition

८६७ ॐ संन्यासिने रमणाय नमः

867 oṃ saṃnyāsine ramaṇāya namaḥ

Om! Prostrations to Ramana, the sanyasin, the renunciate

८६८ ॐ सभानाथाय रमणाय नमः

868 oṃ sabhā-nāthāya ramaṇāya namaḥ

Om! Prostrations to Ramana, who presides over the assembly

८६९ ॐ समदृशे रमणाय नमः

869 oṃ sama-dṛśe ramaṇāya namaḥ

Om! Prostrations to Ramana, who looks upon things equally

८७० ॐ समभावाय रमणाय नमः

870 oṃ sama-bhāvāya ramaṇāya namaḥ

Om! Prostrations to Ramana of equal conviction

८७१ ॐ समाय रमणाय नमः

871 oṃ samāya ramaṇāya namaḥ

Om! Prostrations to Ramana, who is equipoised

८७२ ॐ समदृष्टये रमणाय नमः

872 oṃ sama-dṛṣṭaye ramaṇāya namaḥ

Om! Prostrations to Ramana of equal vision

८७३ ॐ समर्थाय रमणाय नमः

873 oṃ samarthāya ramaṇāya namaḥ

Om! Prostrations to Ramana, who is smart

८७४ ॐ समाधानतत्पराय रमणाय नमः

874 oṃ samādhāna-tatparāya ramaṇāya namaḥ

Om! Prostrations to Ramana, who is intent on peace

८७५ ॐ समानाधिकवर्जिताय रमणाय नमः

875 oṃ samān-ādhika-varjitāya ramaṇāya namaḥ

Om! Prostrations to Ramana without an equal or superior

८७६ ॐ समाधिगताय रमणाय नमः

876 oṃ samādhi-gatāya ramaṇāya namaḥ

Om! Prostrations to Ramana, who has gone into samadhi

८७७ ॐ समाधिनिपुणाय रमणाय नमः

877 oṃ samādhi-nipuṇāya ramaṇāya namaḥ

Om! Prostrations to Ramana, who is an expert in samadhi

८७८ ॐ समाधिसर्वज्ञाय रमणाय नमः

878 oṃ samādhi-sarvajñāya ramaṇāya namaḥ

Om! Prostrations to Ramana, who knows all about samadhi

८७९ ॐ समाधिबहुविधव्याख्याताय रमणाय नमः

879 oṃ samādhi-bahu-vidha-vyākhyātāya ramaṇāya namaḥ

Om! Prostrations to Ramana, who gives exposition on various types of samadhi-s

८८० ॐ सद्भक्तवृन्दपरिवृताय रमणाय नमः

880 oṃ sadbhakta-vṛnda-parivṛtāya ramaṇāya namaḥ

Om! Prostrations to Ramana, who is surrounded by true devotees, devotees of Truth

८८१ ॐ सहजसमाधिने रमणाय नमः

881 oṃ sahaja-samādhine ramaṇāya namaḥ

Om! Prostrations to Ramana, who is in sahaja samadhi

८८२ ॐ सर्वस्मै रमणाय नमः

882 oṃ sarvasmai ramaṇāya namaḥ

Om! Prostrations to Ramana, who is all

८८३ ॐ सर्वज्ञाय रमणाय नमः

883 oṃ sarvajñāya ramaṇāya namaḥ

Om! Prostrations to Ramana, who knows all

८८४ ॐ सर्वयोगिने रमणाय नमः

884 oṃ sarva-yogine ramaṇāya namaḥ

Om! Prostrations to Ramana, who knows all yoga-s

८८५ ॐ सर्वसहायाय रमणाय नमः

885 oṃ sarva-sahāyāya ramaṇāya namaḥ

Om! Prostrations to Ramana, the helper of all

८८६ ॐ सर्वमङ्गलाय रमणाय नमः

886 oṃ sarva-maṅgalāya ramaṇāya namaḥ

Om! Prostrations to Ramana, the all auspicious

८८७ ॐ सर्वमङ्गलकराय रमणाय नमः

887 oṃ sarva-maṅgalakarāya ramaṇāya namaḥ

Om! Prostrations to Ramana, who confers all auspiciousness

८८८ ॐ सर्वकालप्रसादाय रमणाय नमः

888 oṃ sarva-kāla-prasādāya ramaṇāya namaḥ

Om! Prostrations to Ramana, who is pleasant at all times

८८९ ॐ सर्वलोकपूज्याय रमणाय नमः

889 oṃ sarva-loka-pūjyāya ramaṇāya namaḥ

Om! Prostrations to Ramana, who is to be worshipped by all the world

८९० ॐ सर्वपूजिताय रमणाय नमः

890 oṃ sarva-pūjitāya ramaṇāya namaḥ

Om! Prostrations to Ramana, who is worshipped by all

८९१ ॐ सर्वशक्तिमूर्तये रमणाय नमः

891 oṃ sarva-śakti-mūrtaye ramaṇāya namaḥ

Om! Prostrations to Ramana, the personification of all power

८९२ ॐ सर्वचारिणे रमणाय नमः

892 oṃ sarva-cāriṇe ramaṇāya namaḥ

Om! Prostrations to Ramana, who moves all over

८९३ ॐ सर्वाधाराय रमणाय नमः

893 oṃ sarvādhārāya ramaṇāya namaḥ

Om! Prostrations to Ramana, who is the support of all

८९४ ॐ सर्वान्तर्यामिने रमणाय नमः

894 oṃ sarvāntaryāmine ramaṇāya namaḥ

Om! Prostrations to Ramana, who is inside all

८९५ ॐ सर्वपावनाय रमणाय नमः

895 oṃ sarva-pāvanāya ramaṇāya namaḥ

Om! Prostrations to Ramana, who is all holy, makes all holy

८९६ ॐ सर्वलक्षणलाक्षिण्याय रमणाय नमः

896 oṃ sarva-lakṣaṇa-lākṣiṇyāya ramaṇāya namaḥ

Om! Prostrations to Ramana related to the marks of all qualities

८९७ ॐ सर्वविद्याप्रियाय रमणाय नमः

897 oṃ sarva-vidyā-priyāya ramaṇāya namaḥ

Om! Prostrations to Ramana, who likes all branches of knowledge

८९८ ॐ सर्वभयहरणाय रमणाय नमः

898 oṃ sarva-bhaya-haraṇāya ramaṇāya namaḥ

Om! Prostrations to Ramana, who removes all fear

८९९ ॐ सर्वरोगनिवारिणे रमणाय नमः

899 oṃ sarva-roga-nivāriṇe ramaṇāya namaḥ

Om! Prostrations to Ramana, who wards off all illness

९०० ॐ सर्वबाधहराय रमणाय नमः

900 oṃ sarva-bādha-harāya ramaṇāya namaḥ

Om! Prostrations to Ramana, who removes all pain

९०१ ॐ सर्वकष्टनिवारिणे रमणाय नमः

901 oṃ sarva-kaṣṭa-nivāriṇe ramaṇāya namaḥ

Om! Prostrations to Ramana, who wards off all difficulties

९०२ ॐ सर्वदुःखप्रशामनाय रमणाय नमः

902 oṃ sarva-duḥkha-praśamanāya ramaṇāya namaḥ

Om! Prostrations to Ramana, who assuages all grief

९०३ ॐ सर्वभूतहितप्रदाय रमणाय नमः

903 oṃ sarva-bhūta-hita-pradāya ramaṇāya namaḥ

Om! Prostrations to Ramana, who gives welfare to all beings

९०४ ॐ सर्वसंघपरित्यागिने रमणाय नमः

904 oṃ sarva-saṃgha-parityāgine ramaṇāya namaḥ

Om! Prostrations to Ramana, who has renounced all company, attachment

९०५ ॐ सर्वोपाधिविनिर्मुक्ताय रमणाय नमः

905 oṃ sarvopādhi-vinirmuktāya ramaṇāya namaḥ

Om! Prostrations to Ramana, who is free from all limitations

९०६ ॐ सर्वमतसम्मताय रमणाय नमः

906 oṃ sarva-mata-sammatāya ramaṇāya namaḥ

Om! Prostrations to Ramana, who accepts all religions

९०७ ॐ सर्वाणिमतस्थानामाराध्याय रमणाय नमः

907 oṃ sarvāṇi-mata-sthānām-ārādhyāya ramaṇāya namaḥ

Om! Prostrations to Ramana, who is to be worshipped by people of all religions

९०८ ॐ सर्वात्मने रमणाय नमः

908 oṃ sarvātmane ramaṇāya namaḥ

Om! Prostrations to Ramana, the Self of all

९०९ ॐ सवित्रे रमणाय नमः

909 oṃ savitre ramaṇāya namaḥ

Om! Prostrations to Ramana, the Sun-god

९१० ॐ साधुजनप्रियाय रमणाय नमः

910 oṃ sādhu-jana-priyāya ramaṇāya namaḥ

Om! Prostrations to Ramana, who is liked by good people

९११ ॐ साधुजनपालकाय रमणाय नमः

911 oṃ sādhu-jana-pālakāya ramaṇāya namaḥ

Om! Prostrations to Ramana, the ruler, the protector of good persons

९१२ ॐ साधुमानसशोभिताय रमणाय नमः

912 oṃ sādhu-mānasa-śobhitāya ramaṇāya namaḥ

Om! Prostrations to Ramana, who shines in the minds of the good

९१३ ॐ सान्द्रकरुणाय रमणाय नमः

913 oṃ sāndra-karuṇāya ramaṇāya namaḥ

Om! Prostrations to Ramana of strong compassion

९१४ ॐ सिद्धाय रमणाय नमः

914 oṃ siddhāya ramaṇāya namaḥ

Om! Prostrations to Ramana, the accomplished, the ready

९१५ ॐ सिद्धार्थाय रमणाय नमः

915 oṃ siddhārthāya ramaṇāya namaḥ

Om! Prostrations to Ramana, who has accomplished the aim

९१६ ॐ सिद्धसहजसमाधिने रमणाय नमः

916 oṃ siddha-sahaja-samādhine ramaṇāya namaḥ

Om! Prostrations to Ramana, who has attained sahaja samadhi

९१७ ॐ सिद्धिरूपाय रमणाय नमः

917 oṃ siddhi-rūpāya ramaṇāya namaḥ

Om! Prostrations to Ramana of the nature of accomplishment, attainment

९१८ ॐ सिद्धेश्वराय रमणाय नमः

918 oṃ siddheśvarāya ramaṇāya namaḥ

Om! Prostrations to Ramana, the Lord of accomplishment

९१९ ॐ सिंहासनसुखासीनाय रमणाय नमः

919 oṃ siṃhāsana-sukhāsīnāya ramaṇāya namaḥ

Om! Prostrations to Ramana, who is comfortably seated on the lion-throne

९२० ॐ सुकुमाराय रमणाय नमः

920 oṃ sukumārāya ramaṇāya namaḥ

Om! Prostrations to Ramana, the youthful one

९२१ ॐ सुखप्रदाय रमणाय नमः

921 oṃ sukha-pradāya ramaṇāya namaḥ

Om! Prostrations to Ramana, who confers happiness

९२२ ॐ सुखाराध्याय रमणाय नमः

922 oṃ sukhārādhyāya ramaṇāya namaḥ

Om! Prostrations to Ramana, who is to be adored in happiness

९२३ ॐ सुखात्मने रमणाय नमः

923 oṃ sukhātmane ramaṇāya namaḥ

Om! Prostrations to Ramana, the happy Self

९२४ ॐ सुन्दरपुत्राय रमणाय नमः

924 oṃ sundara-putrāya ramaṇāya namaḥ

Om! Prostrations to Ramana, the son of Lord Sundara

९२५ ॐ सुन्दरार्यतपःफलाय रमणाय नमः

925 oṃ sundarārya-tapaḥ-phalāya ramaṇāya namaḥ

Om! Prostrations to Ramana, the fruit of tapas of the revered Sundara

९२६ ॐ सुदर्शनाय रमणाय नमः

926 oṃ sudarśanāya ramaṇāya namaḥ

Om! Prostrations to Ramana of good looks

९२७ ॐ सुप्रतिष्ठाय रमणाय नमः

927 oṃ supratiṣṭāya ramaṇāya namaḥ

Om! Prostrations to Ramana, who is well established

९२८ ॐ सुप्रत्युत्तराय रमणाय नमः

928 oṃ supratyuttarāya ramaṇāya namaḥ

Om! Prostrations to Ramana, who gives good replies

९२९ ॐ सुप्रदीपाय रमणाय नमः

929 oṃ supradīpāya ramaṇāya namaḥ

Om! Prostrations to Ramana, who is shining very brightly

९३० ॐ सुप्रसन्नाय रमणाय नमः

930 oṃ suprasannāya ramaṇāya namaḥ

Om! Prostrations to Ramana, whose presence is pleasant

९३१ ॐ सुमनोहराय रमणाय नमः

931 oṃ sumanoharāya ramaṇāya namaḥ

Om! Prostrations to Ramana, who well captivates the mind

९३२ ॐ सुलभाय रमणाय नमः

932 oṃ sulabhāya ramaṇāya namaḥ

Om! Prostrations to Ramana, who is easy of access

९३३ ॐ सुरूपाय रमणाय नमः

933 oṃ surūpāya ramaṇāya namaḥ

Om! Prostrations to Ramana of excellent nature

९३४ ॐ सुशोभिताय रमणाय नमः

934 oṃ suśobhitāya ramaṇāya namaḥ

Om! Prostrations to Ramana, who shines exceedingly

९३५ ॐ सुहृदाय रमणाय नमः

935 oṃ suhṛdāya ramaṇāya namaḥ

Om! Prostrations to Ramana, who is a close friend

९३६ ॐ सुगन्धिने रमणाय नमः

936 oṃ sugandhine ramaṇāya namaḥ

Om! Prostrations to Ramana exuding fragrance

९३७ ॐ सुवर्चसाय रमणाय नमः

937 oṃ suvarcasāya ramaṇāya namaḥ

Om! Prostrations to Ramana of great power

९३८ ॐ सुभाषिणे रमणाय नमः

938 oṃ subhāṣiṇe ramaṇāya namaḥ

Om! Prostrations to Ramana, who speaks of good things

९३९ ॐ सूत्रात्मने रमणाय नमः

939 oṃ sūtrātmane ramaṇāya namaḥ

Om! Prostrations to Ramana, the Self running through all beings (like a string)

९४० ॐ सेव्याय रमणाय नमः

940 oṃ sevyāya ramaṇāya namaḥ

Om! Prostrations to Ramana, who is to be worshipped

९४१ ॐ सौम्याय रमणाय नमः

941 oṃ saumyāya ramaṇāya namaḥ

Om! Prostrations to Ramana, who is like the moon

९४२ ॐ सौन्दर्यात्मजाय रमणाय नमः

942 oṃ saundaryātmajāya ramaṇāya namaḥ

Om! Prostrations to Ramana, the son of the Devi of beauty

९४३ ॐ सौन्दर्यम्मानन्दनाय रमणाय नमः

943 oṃ saundaryammā-nandanāya ramaṇāya namaḥ

Om! Prostrations to Ramana, the son who delights the lady Azhagamma (Saundaryamma)

९४४ ॐ स्कन्दावताराय रमणाय नमः

944 oṃ skandāvatārāya ramaṇāya namaḥ

Om! Prostrations to Ramana, Skanda in incarnation

९४५ ॐ स्कन्दाश्रमवासाय रमणाय नमः

945 oṃ skandāśrama-vāsāya ramaṇāya namaḥ

Om! Prostrations to Ramana, the resident in Skandashrama

९४६ ॐ स्तेनसाहससहिष्णवे रमणाय नमः

946 oṃ stena-sāhasa-sahiṣṇave ramaṇāya namaḥ

Om! Prostrations to Ramana, who was patient with the high-handedness of the thieves

९४७ ॐ स्तव्याय रमणाय नमः

947 oṃ stavyāya ramaṇāya namaḥ

Om! Prostrations to Ramana, who is to be praised in hymns

९४८ ॐ स्थिराय रमणाय नमः

948 oṃ sthirāya ramaṇāya namaḥ

Om! Prostrations to Ramana, who is fixed, unmoving

९४९ ॐ स्थितप्रज्ञाय रमणाय नमः

949 oṃ sthita-prajñāya ramaṇāya namaḥ

Om! Prostrations to Ramana, who is steadfast in Knowledge

९५० ॐ स्मरणाद्बन्धमोचनाय रमणाय नमः

950 oṃ smaraṇād-bandha-mocanāya ramaṇāya namaḥ

Om! Prostrations to Ramana, who delivers from bondage by mere remembrance [of him]

९५१ ॐ स्वराजे रमणाय नमः

951 oṃ svarāje ramaṇāya namaḥ

Om! Prostrations to Ramana, who shines by himself, monarch of himself

९५२ ॐ स्वच्छाय रमणाय नमः

952 oṃ svacchāya ramaṇāya namaḥ

Om! Prostrations to Ramana, the pellucid

९५३ ॐ स्वप्रकाशाय रमणाय नमः

953 oṃ svaprakāśāya ramaṇāya namaḥ

Om! Prostrations to Ramana, who is self-luminous

९५४ ॐ स्वस्तिमते रमणाय नमः

954 oṃ svastimate ramaṇāya namaḥ

Om! Prostrations to Ramana, who has success, prosperity, well-being

९५५ ॐ स्वस्तिदाय रमणाय नमः

955 oṃ svastidāya ramaṇāya namaḥ

Om! Prostrations to Ramana, who gives success, prosperity, well-being

९५६ ॐ स्वतन्त्राय रमणाय नमः

956 oṃ svatantrāya ramaṇāya namaḥ

Om! Prostrations to Ramana, who is free, independent

९५७ ॐ स्वभावमधुराय रमणाय नमः

957 oṃ svabhāva-madhurāya ramaṇāya namaḥ

Om! Prostrations to Ramana, who is, by nature, sweet

९५८ ॐ स्वामिने रमणाय नमः

958 oṃ svāmine ramaṇāya namaḥ

Om! Prostrations to Ramana, the Svami, the Master

९५९ ॐ हार्दविद्याप्रकाशकाय रमणाय नमः

959 oṃ hārda-vidyā-prakāśakāya ramaṇāya namaḥ

Om! Prostrations to Ramana, who reveals the knowledge of the heart

९६० ॐ हितभाषिणे रमणाय नमः

960 oṃ hita-bhāṣiṇe ramaṇāya namaḥ

Om! Prostrations to Ramana of comforting speech, one who talks of what is beneficial

९६१ ॐ हितकृते रमणाय नमः

961 oṃ hita-kṛte ramaṇāya namaḥ

Om! Prostrations to Ramana, who acts beneficially

९६२ ॐ हितोपदेशाय रमणाय नमः

962 oṃ hitopadeśāya ramaṇāya namaḥ

Om! Prostrations to Ramana, who gives upadesa (instruction) that is beneficial

९६३ ॐ हिरण्यबाहवे रमणाय नमः

963 oṃ hiraṇya-bāhave ramaṇāya namaḥ

Om! Prostrations to Ramana with the golden hand

९६४ ॐ हृदयवेद्याय रमणाय नमः

964 oṃ hṛdaya-vedyāya ramaṇāya namaḥ

Om! Prostrations to Ramana, who is to be known by the heart

९६५ ॐ हृदयग्रन्थिविभेदिने रमणाय नमः

965 oṃ hṛdaya-granthi-vibhedine ramaṇāya namaḥ

Om! Prostrations to Ramana, who cuts asunder the knot of the heart

९६६ ॐ हस्तामलकप्रदर्शकाय रमणाय नमः

966 oṃ hastāmalaka-pradarśakāya ramaṇāya namaḥ

Om! Prostrations to Ramana, who reveals Hastamalaka

९६७ ॐ क्षमायुक्ताय रमणाय नमः

967 oṃ kṣamā-yuktāya ramaṇāya namaḥ

Om! Prostrations to Ramana, who has patience

९६८ ॐ क्षमाधराय रमणाय नमः

968 oṃ kṣamā-dharāya ramaṇāya namaḥ

Om! Prostrations to Ramana, who carries forgiveness, supports the world

९६९ ॐ क्षयवृद्धिविनिर्मुक्ताय रमणाय नमः

969 oṃ kṣaya-vṛddhi-vinirmuktāya ramaṇāya namaḥ

Om! Prostrations to Ramana, who is free of decay and growth

९७० ॐ क्षितिसमक्षमाय रमणाय नमः

970 oṃ kṣiti-sama-kṣamāya ramaṇāya namaḥ

Om! Prostrations to Ramana, who is patient like the earth

९७१ ॐ क्षयादिरहिताय रमणाय नमः

971 oṃ kṣayādi-rahitāya ramaṇāya namaḥ

Om! Prostrations to Ramana, who is devoid of decay and such

९७२ ॐ क्षेत्रज्ञाय रमणाय नमः

972 oṃ kṣetra-jñāya ramaṇāya namaḥ

Om! Prostrations to Ramana, who is the knower of the field

९७३ ॐ ज्ञानसंबन्धस्वरूपाय रमणाय नमः

973 oṃ jñānasaṃbandha-svarūpāya ramaṇāya namaḥ

Om! Prostrations to Ramana of the nature of saint Jnanasambandha

९७४ ॐ ज्ञानस्वरूपाय रमणाय नमः

974 oṃ jñāna-svarūpāya ramaṇāya namaḥ

Om! Prostrations to Ramana of the nature of Knowledge

९७५ ॐ ज्ञानमूर्तये रमणाय नमः

975 oṃ jñāna-mūrtaye ramaṇāya namaḥ

Om! Prostrations to Ramana, who is the embodiment of Knowledge

९७६ ॐ ज्ञानचक्षुषे रमणाय नमः

976 oṃ jñāna-cakṣuṣe ramaṇāya namaḥ

Om! Prostrations to Ramana, who has the eye of Knowledge

९७७ ॐ ज्ञानदीपाय रमणाय नमः

977 oṃ jñāna-dīpāya ramaṇāya namaḥ

Om! Prostrations to Ramana, who is the lamp of Knowledge

९७८ ॐ ज्ञानबोधकाय रमणाय नमः

978 oṃ jñāna-bodhakāya ramaṇāya namaḥ

Om! Prostrations to Ramana, who is the teacher of Knowledge

९७९ ॐ ज्ञानप्रकाशाय रमणाय नमः

979 oṃ jñāna-prakāśāya ramaṇāya namaḥ

Om! Prostrations to Ramana, who is the effulgence of Knowledge

९८० ॐ ज्ञानानन्दाय रमणाय नमः

980 oṃ jñān-ānandāya ramaṇāya namaḥ

Om! Prostrations to Ramana, who is the bliss of Knowledge

९८१ ॐ ज्ञानार्णवाय रमणाय नमः

981 oṃ jñān-ārṇavāya ramaṇāya namaḥ

Om! Prostrations to Ramana, who is an ocean of Knowledge

९८२ ॐ ज्ञानशक्तये रमणाय नमः

982 oṃ jñāna-śaktaye ramaṇāya namaḥ

Om! Prostrations to Ramana, who is the power of Knowledge

९८३ ॐ ज्ञानगम्याय रमणाय नमः

983 oṃ jñāna-gamyāya ramaṇāya namaḥ

Om! Prostrations to Ramana, who is to be reached by Knowledge

९८४ ॐ ज्ञानसिद्धिदाय रमणाय नमः

984 oṃ jñāna-siddhi-dāya ramaṇāya namaḥ

Om! Prostrations to Ramana, who confers attainment of Knowledge

९८५ ॐ ज्ञानसाम्राज्यदायिने रमणाय नमः

985 oṃ jñāna-sāmrājya-dāyine ramaṇāya namaḥ

Om! Prostrations to Ramana, who confers the empire of Knowledge

९८६ ॐ ज्ञानभास्कराय रमणाय नमः

986 oṃ jñāna-bhāskarāya ramaṇāya namaḥ

Om! Prostrations to Ramana, the sun of Knowledge

९८७ ॐ ज्ञानावताराय रमणाय नमः

987 oṃ jñānāvatārāya ramaṇāya namaḥ

Om! Prostrations to Ramana, the incarnation of Knowledge

९८८ ॐ ज्ञानेश्वराय रमणाय नमः

988 oṃ jñāneśvarāya ramaṇāya namaḥ

Om! Prostrations to Ramana, the Lord of Knowledge

९८९ ॐ एकस्मै रमणाय नमः

989 oṃ ekasmai ramaṇāya namaḥ

Om! Prostrations to Ramana, the One

९९० ॐ द्वैतवर्जिताय रमणाय नमः

990 oṃ dvaita-varjitāya ramaṇāya namaḥ

Om! Prostrations to Ramana, who is devoid of "two" (duality)

९९१ ॐ त्रिपुटीजगज्जीवपरादिरहिताय रमणाय नमः

991 oṃ tripuṭī-jagaj-jīva-parādi-rahitāya ramaṇāya namaḥ

Om! Prostrations to Ramana, who is beyond the triad of jagat-jiva-para (world, individual and the Supreme) and such

९९२ ॐ चतुष्टयान्तःकरणमनोबुध्यहंकारचित्तातीताय रमणाय नमः

992 oṃ catuṣṭay-āntaḥkaraṇa-mano-buddhy-ahaṃkāra-citt-ātītāya ramaṇāya namaḥ

Om! Prostrations to Ramana, who transcends the quadrad of inner senses, mind-intellect-ego-thought

९९३ ॐ पञ्चेन्द्रियप्राणकोशादिपराय रमणाय नमः

993 oṃ pañcendriya-prāṇa-kośādi-parāya ramaṇāya namaḥ

Om! Prostrations to Ramana, who is beyond the pentad of senses, prana-s, sheaths and such

९९४ ॐ षड्रिपुवर्गकामक्रोधादि निग्रहाय रमणाय नमः

994 oṃ ṣaḍ-ripu-varga-kāma-krodhādi nigrahāya ramaṇāya namaḥ

Om! Prostrations to Ramana, who has conquered the sextet of enemies such as desire, anger and such

९९५ ॐ सप्तसप्तितेजसे रमणाय नमः

995 oṃ sapta-sapti-tejase ramaṇāya namaḥ

Om! Prostrations to Ramana, who has the brilliance of the Sun, with seven horses

९९६ ॐ अष्टाङ्गज्ञानविद्याप्रयोगविवरणाय रमणाय नमः

996 oṃ aṣṭāṅga-jñāna-vidyā-prayoga-vivaraṇāya ramaṇāya namaḥ

Om! Prostrations to Ramana, who gives an exposition of, explains the application of, the Knowledge of eightfold parts

९९७ ॐ नवरसनिराकृताखण्डैकरसाय रमणाय नमः

997 oṃ nava-rasa-nirākṛt-ākhaṇḍaika-rasāya ramaṇāya namaḥ

Om! Prostrations to Ramana, who has the One undivided essence, rejecting the nine rasa-s

९९८ ॐ दशशतमधुरपुण्यनाम्ने रमणाय नमः

998 oṃ daśa-śata-madhura-puṇya-nāmne ramaṇāya namaḥ

Om! Prostrations to Ramana, who has a decad of centuries of sweet holy names

९९९ ॐ नामरूपातीताय रमणाय नमः

999 oṃ nāma-rūp-ātītāya ramaṇāya namaḥ

Om! Prostrations to Ramana, who transcends name and form

१००० ॐ परस्मै ब्रह्मणे रमणाय नमः

1000 oṃ parasmai brahmaṇe ramaṇāya namaḥ

Om! Prostrations to Ramana, the Supreme Brahman

ॐ

For a complete list of books on Advaita Vedanta and the Teachings of Sri Ramana Maharshi, or to reach Nome, please contact the publisher:

SAT

SOCIETY OF ABIDANCE IN TRUTH

1834 OCEAN STREET, SANTA CRUZ, CALIFORNIA 95060

(831) 425-7287 ~ www.SATRamana.org ~ sat@satramana.org

www.ingramcontent.com/pod-product-compliance
Lightning Source LLC
Chambersburg PA
CBHW041127110526
44592CB00020B/2712
* 9 7 8 1 9 4 7 1 5 4 3 2 2 *